From Junior to Senior College

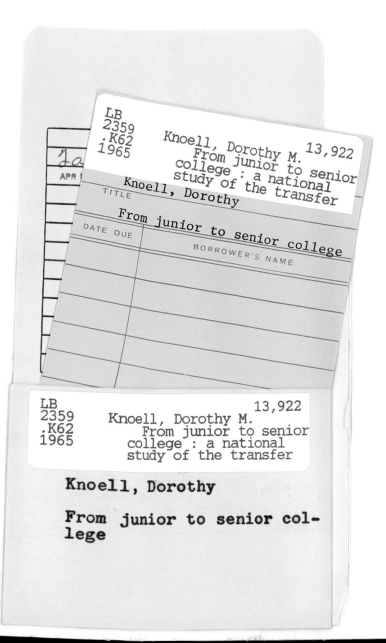

Joint Committee on Junior and Senior Colleges[1]

AMERICAN ASSOCIATION OF JUNIOR COLLEGES

JAMES L. WATTENBARGER, Director, Division of Community Junior Colleges, Florida State Department of Education; *Chairman*

EDMUND J. GLEAZER, JR., Executive Director, American Association of Junior Colleges; *Secretary and ex officio member*

PETER MASIKO, JR., President, Miami-Dade Junior College

EDWARD W. SEAY, President, Centenary College for Women

AMERICAN ASSOCIATION OF COLLEGIATE REGISTRARS AND ADMISSIONS OFFICERS

CHARLES E. HARRELL, Registrar, Indiana University; *ex officio*

ROBERT G. SAWYER, Director of Admissions, Colby Junior College

R. F. THOMASON,[2] Dean of Admissions and Records, University of Tennessee

CLYDE VROMAN, Director of Admissions, University of Michigan

ASSOCIATION OF AMERICAN COLLEGES

GEORGE H. ARMACOST, President, University of Redlands

LLOYD M. BERTHOLF, President, Illinois Wesleyan University

FREDERICK DEW. BOLMAN, JR.,[3] President, Franklin and Marshall College

CARTER DAVIDSON,[4] President, Association of American Colleges; *ex officio* (deceased)

THEODORE A. DISTLER,[4] Executive Director, Association of American Colleges; *ex officio*

H. ELLIS FINGER,[5] President, Millsaps College

THOMAS A. SPRAGENS,[5] President, Centre College of Kentucky

[1] The positions of the members are those occupied at the time of appointment to the committee.

[2] Former member, now deceased.

[3] Former chairman of commitee, now Director of Special Programs, Esso Education Foundation.

[4] Carter Davidson replaced Dr. Distler upon the latter's retirement in 1965.

[5] Thomas A. Spragens replaced Dr. Finger on the committee in 1965, when the latter left the college.

From Junior to Senior College:

A National Study of the Transfer Student

By
Dorothy M. Knoell
and
Leland L. Medsker
Center for the Study of Higher Education
University of California, Berkeley

Published for

Joint Committee on Junior and Senior Colleges

by

American Council on Education

Third impression, March, 1969

Printed in the United States of America

Foreword

INCREASINGLY, the community college is the means by which states are equalizing and expanding educational opportunity beyond the high school. Some state universities and state colleges have raised their standards for admission, which means that students of lesser ability must turn to community colleges in the public educational system. For example, the University of California and the California State Colleges now accept only students in the upper eighth and third, respectively, of their high school graduating classes. Furthermore, the University of California and the California State Colleges encourage students to take the first two years of a four-year program in the community colleges. The University of Illinois recently limited for the first time the number of freshmen accepted. At the same time, Illinois adopted a statewide master plan which included a proposal for the establishment of many new community colleges. New universities or university campuses and new state colleges are also being created in various states, but it is obvious that two-year institutions will have to carry the greater part of the load of students during the enrollment bulge.

If education beyond the fourteenth year is to be assured to students whose aptitude and achievement qualify them for it, community colleges, in addition to their several other functions, will have to prepare students for successful work in the upper divisions of four-year institutions. The importance of the transfer function of community colleges led the Center for the Study of Higher Education, under the direction of Dr. Dorothy M. Knoell and Dr. Leland L. Medsker, to make a nationwide study of the performance of transfer students, and to study the articulation between two-year and four-year colleges.[1] The center is indebted to a joint advisory committee

[1] Dorothy M. Knoell and Leland L. Medsker, *Factors Affecting Performance of Students from Two- to Four-Year Colleges* and *Articulation Between Two-Year and Four-Year Colleges* (Berkeley: Center for the Study of Higher Education, University of California, 1964).

comprised of representatives from the Association of American Colleges, the American Association of Collegiate Registrars and Admissions Officers, and the American Association of Junior Colleges for its assistance in designing and guiding the research.

A grant from the Esso Education Foundation made it possible for the American Association of Junior Colleges to hold state conferences on the results of these studies and the implications of the findings for admission, counseling, curriculum, instruction, and institutional articulation for both two-year colleges and senior institutions. The conferences were attended by representatives of both the junior and the senior colleges and of appropriate state coordinating agencies. The interest of the participants at these conferences made it apparent that a summary of the Knoell–Medsker investigations should be prepared for wide distribution. Fortunately, the American Council on Education has undertaken the publication and distribution of this document.

There is no need to paraphrase here the characteristics and findings of the studies. It may be worthwhile to point out, however, that the national transfer study involved some 10,000 students, 345 two-year institutions which they entered as freshmen, and a diverse group of forty-three senior colleges and universities to which they transferred. The prediction of success of the transfer student turned out to be a complicated problem. His academic performance in the four-year college or university was the outcome of a subtle accommodation between his attributes and the characteristics of the institution he entered or the particular part of the institution in which he concentrated his studies. The success of the transfer student was a function of his characteristics, the range of alternatives open to him when he chose a senior institution, the academic standards and the total climate of the senior college to which he transferred, and the interaction between the characteristics of the student and the institution. This finding has significant implications for the assessment of individual characteristics; the definition and dissemination of the attributes of four-year institutions; the counseling, admission, and academic placement of students; and finally, the articulation and coordination between particular institutions. These are some of the problems to which Knoell and Medsker have addressed themselves in this summary of their investigations.

T. R. McCONNELL, *Chairman*
Center for the Study of Higher Education

Contents

List of Tables

Significance
of the Transfer Function

A CONSERVATIVE estimate of the junior college role in the national enrollment pattern places one in four first-time students in some type of two-year institution—a traditional junior college, a comprehensive community college, a university extension center, or a technical institute. In California, where about 80 percent of the high school graduates reside in junior college districts, as many as three new freshmen in five are entering the seventy-five or more public junior colleges which are now offering lower division programs. The proportion will most certainly increase in the next decade, both in California and nationally, as more states develop new community college systems, as existing two-year colleges and systems are strengthened, and as four-year institutions become at the same time more selective and more costly to students. While it now seems unlikely that senior colleges and universities will soon, if ever, abandon their freshman classes completely, the trend toward enrolling a high proportion of new freshmen in local two-year colleges seems irreversible.

The present decade in higher education is distinguished by a greatly accelerated effort to expand opportunity for education beyond the high school. Many state master plans now include proposals both for achieving greater coordination of higher education at the state level and for developing (or strengthening) the two-year colleges. In state after state the junior college has been seized upon as the most likely institution for achieving the twofold goal of expanding educational opportunity and conserving the state's economic and other resources. This need to conserve while expanding is quite apparent from long-range estimates of the numbers of students who will want to attend college, the size of the faculties

1

needed to teach them, the scope of the building program to house them, and the cost of the total enterprise. Master planners aspire to have a low-cost, open-door community college within the reach of nearly all high school graduates by the early 1970's. They want an institution that will be committed to serving the broad educational needs of the local communities. The planners make the assumption, at least tacitly, that there will continue to be ample opportunity for qualified junior college graduates to transfer to four-year institutions to complete their degree programs and that articulation between and among the two types of institutions will be easily accomplished.

Need for an Educational Model

New institutions and whole new systems of colleges are being created to meet the increased demand for higher education without benefit of a comprehensive model of a system of higher education against which to test the effectiveness of particular types of institutions in achieving societal goals. The assumption tends to be made that "more is better," i.e., increased opportunity for higher education will automatically produce a better educated citizenry. Little attempt has been made until now to study the flow of students through secondary school into different types of colleges and universities, among and through collegiate institutions to different levels and degrees, in different state subsystems, and under different types of organization of higher education. While statistical information about access to college at the freshman level is improving, very little is yet known about the mobility of students after they first enroll in college—mobility between institutions, overseas, into off-campus programs of study, and from level to level.

The focus is now rightfully on the junior college in the higher education model as the institution which increasing numbers of college freshmen will enter on their way to achieving a wide spectrum of educational and occupational objectives. Many newly attracted students would not have attended college at all if a low-cost, open-door junior college had not been within commuting distance. To these will be added the students who are being diverted from existing four-year institutions as a result of higher freshman admission standards and increased costs of attending college. The net effect will be increased heterogeneity in the junior college population to be served and, at the same time, increased homogeneity in the lower division population of the four-year colleges.

The new comprehensive community college is, of course, a multi-function institution serving not only recent high school graduates but also adults whose previous education ranges from less than high school completion to a baccalaureate degree and beyond. Transfer programs now attract the largest proportion of junior college students, particularly among recent high school graduates. However, technical-vocational curricula leading to immediate employment are also attracting large numbers of students, as are terminal liberal arts programs and adult education offerings. The effective community college offers post-high-school instruction of high quality and at the same time serves the equally important function of guidance for the very large segment of students who have not yet tested their interests and capabilities sufficiently to embark upon employment or on baccalaureate degree programs.

The junior college population in the aggregate probably resembles the high school graduating class with respect to both academic ability and socioeconomic characteristics, although there are fewer junior college students at the extremes in both these dimensions than are found in the total age group.[1] There are the high school under-achievers who are taking advantage of one more chance to demonstrate their ability to do satisfactory college work; the late deciders about college attendance who have high school deficiencies; the immature who are emotionally and intellectually unready to enter a four-year college; the insufficiently motivated and the uncertain; and the capable students who lack financial backing for college attendance away from home or who simply want to attend what may be a smaller, less formal college for their first two years.

The net effect of junior college development on the production of baccalaureate recipients has scarcely been considered in making master plans. Logic dictates that an increase in the number of high school graduates entering any type of college will bring about an increase in the gross number of baccalaureate degrees produced. However, there are those who fear that the best students may become disillusioned by higher education in the junior college and that the less able transfer students from junior college will be unable to compete in a four-year institution.[2]

[1] Leland L. Medsker, "The Junior College Student," one of a series of papers to be published by the Committee for the Appraisal and Development of Junior College Student Personnel Programs, a project supported by the Carnegie Corporation of New York in a grant to the American Association of Junior Colleges (page 10 of the mimeographed paper).

[2] There is some, as yet unpublished, evidence that California has one of the nation's highest percentages of high school graduates attending college, but at the same time its percentage of baccalaureate-degree recipients in the college-age group is below the national average. The large proportion of lower

The study of the success of transfer students from two-year colleges which is reported here is but one small part of the research which is needed on the flow of students through the higher education system. Its importance rests on the fact that an increasing number of students are taking their lower division work in two-year institutions, and on the need for a large percentage of the work force to be trained at the baccalaureate degree level. The research sheds no light on the comparative incidence of attrition among lower division students of equal ability who enter the two types of colleges as freshmen. Information still needs to be obtained about attrition both during the first two years of college and between the sophomore and junior years when students normally transfer and/or enter upper division programs.

In spite of this limitation in scope, a study of transfer student performance should contribute significantly to an understanding of this one major subsystem of the higher education model—the junior college as a *transfer* institution. If the two-year colleges do not prepare students to achieve their baccalaureate degree goals at some acceptable level of performance, the effectiveness of the entire subsystem will be seriously open to question. Transfer student performance may be thought of as a more critical test of the subsystem than the mere flow of students through junior college into four-year institutions, since transfer is relatively pointless if students have a low probability of succeeding in the upper division.

Scope of the Transfer Study

The primary goal of the transfer study was to obtain facts, figures, and opinions leading to a fairly comprehensive evaluation of the junior college transfer function as it was being performed in the early 1960's. The following assumptions were made:

1. Students going to junior college are probably different from those attending four-year institutions as freshmen, in their socioeconomic characteristics, intellectual disposition, occupational interests, and ability to do college work.

2. Junior college grading standards may (and perhaps should) be different from those of many four-year colleges because of differences in the students whom they serve and in the objectives they are expected to achieve.

3. The junior college should not be a carbon copy of the lower

---

division students enrolled in junior college is believed to be a factor in this seeming discrepancy.

division of the state university or any other four-year institution. Instead, each junior college should create the best possible program to prepare transfer students for upper division work in a multiplicity of four-year institutions, and to give those students who do not transfer a general education experience of high quality.

The rather immediate objectives which dictated the design of the transfer study are these:

1. To find out what junior college students are like—for example, their personal and family characteristics, economic resources, age, interests, abilities, and experiences—and to learn how these students made their educational plans and decisions.

2. To learn as much as possible about their performance in junior college and after transfer—their grades, patterns of attendance, academic penalties and awards, and, most important of all, what their degree status was at the beginning of the fourth year after transfer, i.e., graduated, still enrolled at the undergraduate level, or dropped out.

3. To compare them with "native" students—those who took all their work at a single four-year institution—using measures of their personal characteristics, academic ability, the grades they earned at different levels, and their patterns of progress through college.

4. To find out which characteristics, traits, and achievements are linked to success after transfer, in terms of the students' earning good grades, persisting in their programs, and graduating on time.

5. To learn whether transfer students are equally successful in all types of four-year colleges and in all states and, if not, why not.

6. To gain a better understanding of attrition among transfer students—the distinctive characteristics of students who drop out, the circumstances under which they do so, and what happens to them afterward.

7. To find out what kinds of admission requirements, credit evaluations, retention policies, and graduation requirements were in effect in the various four-year colleges both in 1960 and in 1964, and to estimate changes and trends which might affect the future mobility of transfer students.

8. To analyze the ways in which the two- and four-year colleges

have been working together on transfer problems, both in voluntary articulation arrangements and in the newer, more formal coordinating agencies.

The transfer study was commissioned by a Joint Committee on Junior and Senior Colleges of the Association of American Colleges, the American Association of Junior Colleges, and the American Association of Collegiate Registrars and Admissions Officers. The committee was established in 1957 to deliberate about transfer problems and practices, and in 1960 it requested the Center for the Study of Higher Education to formulate an appropriate research proposal, to secure the necessary funding, and to carry out the research. The Cooperative Research Branch of the U.S. Office of Education supported the research with two successive grants, with the committee serving in an advisory capacity throughout the study. Two technical research reports were published by the center at the conclusion of the project.[3] In late 1964 the Esso Education Foundation made a grant to the American Association of Junior Colleges for a series of state and regional conferences leading to the development of a set of guidelines for transfer which the three sponsoring associations will be asked to adopt at their 1966 annual meetings.

Related Research

Earlier studies of junior college transfer students yielded findings which may be summarized briefly as follows:[4]

1. Junior college students usually experience some drop in grade point average in their first term after transfer, below the cumulative average they earned in junior college. The grades of the students who persist in the four-year colleges generally improve in successive terms after transfer.

2. Junior college students often do less well than native students in their first term in the upper division, but the differential between the two groups decreases in successive terms.

---

[3] Dorothy M. Knoell and Leland L. Medsker, *Factors Affecting Performance of Transfer Students from Two- to Four-Year Colleges: With Implications for Coordination and Articulation* and *Articulation Between Two-Year and Four-Year Colleges* (Berkeley: Center for the Study of Higher Education, University of California, 1964).

[4] Grace V. Bird, "Preparation for Advanced Study," *The Public Junior College,* Fifty-fifth Yearbook of the National Society for the Study of Education (Chicago: The University of Chicago Press, 1956), LV, Part I.

Leland L. Medsker, *The Junior College: Progress and Prospect* (New York: McGraw-Hill Book Company, 1960).

Selection and Retention of Students in California's Public Institutions of Higher Education (Sacramento: California State Department of Education, 1961).

3. Attrition tends to be higher for junior college transfer students in the upper division than for native students who persist to the junior year.

4. Junior college transfer students often require more time than native students to complete their baccalaureate degree programs.

Several major studies of the flow of students in higher education are in various stages of completion. Among these is Project Talent which involves a follow-up of high school graduates in 1960 and for several subsequent years, many of whom entered junior colleges and later transferred to four-year institutions. Likewise, certain studies are now under way at the Center for the Study of Higher Education at Berkeley which are focused on the flow of students through college. Several of them involve students who first enrolled in junior colleges. Thus, in the near future findings from other longitudinal studies will supplement the data from the project reported here and should facilitate decision-making about such matters as planning educational systems, articulating college programs, and counseling students.

Overview of This Volume

A brief description of the samples studied, data collected, procedures followed, and the general findings of the transfer study will be given in the second chapter. Subsequent chapters will contain detailed findings on student performance, individual and group factors affecting performance, curriculum problems, counseling and other student personnel services, policies affecting transfer students, and articulation and coordination. The major conclusions and their implications appear in the final chapter.

2

Nature
of the Transfer Study

IN one sense the transfer study is the story of what happened to one large group of junior college students who enrolled in baccalaureate degree programs in many different four-year colleges and universities. In another sense it is an account of articulation and coordination among colleges in states with some type of system of public junior colleges in 1960.

The core group on which the study was focused included 7,243 junior college students who transferred in 1960 to forty-three four-year colleges and universities in ten states. Sampling began with the selection of states in which the study was to be carried on. In most states all institutions which admitted one hundred or more junior college transfer students in 1960 were invited to participate, together with some which admitted fewer than one hundred. No specification was made of the type or location of the junior colleges from which the students came, nor of when the students may have enrolled in junior college. The students represented a total of 345 two-year institutions located in forty-three states and the Canal Zone. However, 70 percent of the junior colleges were located in the ten states which were selected for study, and 91 percent of the students transferred from an in-state junior college.

The sample of states was limited to ten on the grounds that a larger number could not be studied firsthand or reported on in depth. However, enrollment statistics for 1960 made it appear quite certain that few, if any, states with very large junior college transfer groups would be overlooked in restricting the sample to ten. Size of junior college enrollment was the first criterion for selecting states. Then an attempt was made to secure broad geographical representation from all parts of the country and to include states with different types of organization and control of higher education. The states selected are California, Florida, Georgia, Illinois, Kansas, Michigan, New York, Pennsylvania, Texas, and Washington. New York and Pennsylvania were included, despite the rather restricted groups which were available for study, as the best representatives of the eastern states. Pennsylvania also provided an opportunity to study one situation in which the two-year colleges are primarily branches of the state university. A number of other types of organization or control are represented by particular states: Georgia, with all public institutions under a single governing board; Michigan and Illinois, with locally controlled junior colleges, several separate governing boards for various state universities, and little coordination among them in 1960; Florida, with the junior colleges a part of the county school system and with the state universities under a single Board of Control; and New York, with the planning and coordination of all education, both public and private, the responsibility of the University of the State of New York. New York State was unique in that it had no land-grant university comparable to those of other states in 1960 but its two-year institutions included both comprehensive community colleges and highly specialized agricultural and technical institutes.

In each state an attempt was made to involve in the study the major state university, several other state institutions, and one or more private institutions. There was no direct involvement of the junior colleges in the selection of institutions, although many were helpful in identifying the most important four-year institutions to be included. None of the invited institutions declined to participate; a few private universities were dropped by mutual consent when a canvass of their records yielded only a small number of full-time junior college students. The participating institutions are listed in Table I, together with the numbers of students who were included in various types of analyses.

These institutions were grouped into five types in the expectation that certain similarities in program, policies, and characteristics would produce a certain communality in transfer student performance. The five types are these: (1) the major state universities (or the public university in each state which has the longest record of university status), (2) public institutions with primary emphasis on the preparation of teachers, (3) other state colleges and universities with multiple functions, (4) private universities, and (5) technical institutions.

The private segment of higher education was undoubtedly underrepresented in the study at both the two-year and four-year college

9

TABLE 1: NUMBERS AND TYPES OF STUDENTS IN THE FOUR-YEAR INSTITUTIONS PARTICIPATING IN THE TRANSFER STUDENT STUDY

INSTITUTIONS BY TYPE	1960 TRANSFERS			1962 GRADUATES		
	Men	Women	Total	Natives	1960 Transfers	Early Transfers
Type 1: Major state universities						
University of California:						
Berkeley Campus	470	146	616	203	252	104
Los Angeles Campus	328	134	462	218	223	77
University of Florida	197	65	262	112	55	61
University of Georgia	238	56	294	133	152	—
University of Illinois	177	41	218	82	55	21
University of Kansas	140	50	190	116	37	64
University of Michigan	147	80	227	139	92	42
Pennsylvania State University	228	41	269	143	158	—
University of Texas	186	69	255	137	85	83
University of Washington	258	65	323	110	75	64
Total	2,369	747	3,116	1,393	1,184	516
Type 2: Teachers colleges						
Georgia Southern College	51	36	87	32	63	22
Kansas State College of Pittsburg	129	66	195	89	84	26
Kansas State Teachers College of Emporia	61	37	98	90	70	26
Central Michigan University	70	53	123	38	53	18
Eastern Michigan University	29	40	69	51	36	22
Western Michigan University	130	73	203	96	84	10
State University of New York:						
College at New Paltz	14	20	34	13	4	7
College at Oswego	40	12	52	47	24	1
Sam Houston State Teachers College	83	34	117	74	70	—
Western Washington State College	95	40	135	61	57	30
Total	702	411	1,113	591	545	162
Type 3: Other state institutions						
Long Beach State College	221	136	357	122	157	51
San Francisco State College	294	197	491	166	169	77
Florida State University	161	83	244	145	149	1

10

TABLE 1—*Continued*

INSTITUTIONS BY TYPE	1960 TRANSFERS			1962 GRADUATES		
	Men	Women	Total	Natives	1960 Transfers	Early Transfers
Type 3 (continued)						
Northern Illinois University	86	43	129	68	70	10
Southern Illinois University	42	18	60	67	29	12
Kansas State University	126	28	154	68	37	—
University of Michigan:						
Dearborn Campus	53	12	65	—	—	—
Flint Campus	39	24	63	—	—	—
Michigan State University	140	54	194	116	112	72
Wayne State University	127	55	182	67	41	76
Texas Technological College	108	44	152	123	58	66
Washington State University	74	24	98	78	35	29
Total	1,471	718	2,189	1,020	857	394
Type 4: Private universities						
University of the Pacific	51	28	79	32	29	11
University of Southern California	122	35	157	80	98	—
University of Miami	54	36	90	34	23	16
Emory University	42	9	51	46	33	8
Loyola University (Illinois)	43	11	54	45	13	5
Roosevelt University	64	17	81	17	25	21
New York University	43	47	90	—	—	—
Seattle University	17	5	22	—	—	—
Total	436	188	624	254	221	61
Type 5: Technical institutions						
Georgia Institute of Technology	51	—	51	25	2	19
Rochester Institute of Technology	76	5	81	38	7	28
Texas A&M University	69	—	69	28	30	—
Total	196	5	201	91	39	47
Grand total	5,174	2,069	7,243	3,349	2,846	1,180

levels. The bias occurred as a result of the design of the study or, to look at it another way, as a result of the differing attendance patterns of students in the private and public sectors. Students from private junior colleges tended to disperse themselves among a very large number of four-year institutions, usually private, while the public junior college students tended to flow into a small number of public institutions in each state. It was thus impossible to obtain appropriate representation from the private sector without expanding the study to include a very large number of states and institutions.[1] However, the smallness of the sample of private colleges was regarded as only a minor limitation in the study, since future growth is expected to take place primarily in the public sector.

The "Who" of the Study

The 1960 Transfers. Although states and four-year institutions within states were sampled, all junior college transfer students who met certain criteria were included in the data collection and analysis. In other words, no sampling of transfer students was made, per se. The major criteria which the participating institutions were instructed to use in identifying students for study were these:

1. The last college the student attended before transfer should have been a junior college (or other two-year institution) and the student should have had at least a full semester's work there. However, he may have attended any number of colleges after graduation from high school. Students with lapses in enrollment after junior college were to be included, as well as those who transferred without a break in enrollment.

2. The transfer student should have entered the participating four-year institution in the fall of 1960 as a full-time student with junior and/or upper division standing. When it was found that a sizeable group of students transferred to some institutions after only one year in junior college, the criterion was modified to include such students whenever institutions were willing to undertake the additional work. Because of the lateness of the modification in the design, the sophomores who were included constituted only 11 percent of the total study group.

[1] A different type of transfer study involving private institutions appears to be needed which would be concerned less with statistical evidence concerning performance and more with the accommodation of small numbers of transfer students in programs which have not been formally articulated with junior college programs.

The number of 1960 transfer students at each institution studied is shown in the first three columns of Table 1. Nearly three-fourths of the students transferred to the twenty state universities in the study—43 percent to what have been called the ten major state universities and 30 percent to the ten other multi-function state institutions. Only 15 percent transferred to the ten teachers colleges, 9 percent to the eight private universities, and 3 percent to the three technical institutions in the study. A common pattern of dispersion among the types of colleges was observed in most of the states—a tendency for students to flow into the large state universities except when they were excluded by selective admission policies. There was considerable imbalance among the states in the numbers of transfer students who participated in the study. California, with its several hundred thousand students in public junior colleges, contributed 30 percent of the transfer students in the study. Michigan students accounted for 16 percent. New York and Pennsylvania, on the other hand, had only 3 and 4 percent, respectively. Each of the remaining six states accounted for about 8 percent of the total. New York appears to have been quite seriously under-represented in the study when its 1959 junior college enrollment is compared with those of other states in relation to their participation in the study. However, there is reason to believe that the percentage of junior college students in New York who transfer to in-state institutions is much smaller than in other states.

Native–Transfer Student Comparisons. To assess the performance of transfer students against that of students who took all their work at a single four-year institution, comparison groups of 4,026 transfers and 3,349 native students were chosen. The figures for each institution are shown in the last three columns of Table 1.

Ideally, in order to make a fair comparison of the two types of students, matched samples in two- and four-year institutions would be identified at the freshman level and followed until most had either graduated or dropped out permanently. Still another appropriate but less tedious procedure would be to identify matched samples of native and transfer students at the time of transfer as juniors or entry into the upper division. However, neither procedure was operationally feasible in the present study—the first because of the obvious factor of time, the second because there is often no clear demarcation between the lower and upper division and because class level has relatively little meaning in this context. It would have been possible to obtain a sample of native students who entered four-year colleges in 1958 and who were still enrolled in 1960, presumably as juniors, when the junior college students transferred.

13

However, such a procedure would have ignored the large number of transfer students who entered junior college before 1958 and progressed slowly through the lower division. A prime consideration in selecting comparison groups was the necessity to terminate the major data collection in 1962.

In light of these considerations, a decision was made to abandon the traditional technique of identifying a sample at some point of intake (or at the beginning of some aspect of program) and, instead, to draw samples of 1962 graduates for comparison purposes. The graduates had entered college at various times, progressed at different rates of speed, and followed various attendance patterns before completing their degree programs. The colleges were asked to estimate the number of junior college transfer students who would complete their degree programs in 1962, *regardless* of their date of transfer, and to draw a sample of native students who were expected to graduate at the same time. The native sample was to be equal in number and with about the same proportions of men and women and distribution of majors as the transfer group.

There were certain advantages to the plan to compare groups of graduates, rather than entering students. One advantage rests on the assumption that the most able students persist through the lower division of each subsystem of higher education, i.e., the junior college and the four-year institution, and continue to graduation. If baccalaureate degree recipients who began their work in a junior college did not compare favorably with those who took all their work in a four-year institution, then there appeared to be little likelihood that other groups of transfer students would compare at all well with native students. Second, no artificial time limit was imposed by comparing graduates, such as that which characterizes most longitudinal studies which move forward in time. Date of enrollment was allowed to vary, thus making it possible to compare attendance patterns, length of time required to complete degree requirements, scholarship actions, and other occurrences in the groups of native and transfer student graduates. Some of the transfer students entered four-year institutions at the sophomore level in 1959 or earlier, others entered as juniors before 1960 but took more than two years to complete their programs, and still others attended somewhat sporadically between the time they transferred and graduation in 1962. Similarly, some native students entered college before 1958 and either took more than four years to complete their programs or withdrew temporarily at some point during their programs.

The major disadvantage in comparing graduates was, of course, the lack of access to information about attrition among native students. However, there is considerable evidence from institutional studies that attrition is quite high during the lower division, particularly in public institutions, and that native students who persist into the upper division have a high probability of graduating. Prior studies of entering native and transfer students have involved gross groups whose composition changed from semester to semester as attrition took place. It is believed that the present study is unique in that fairly intact groups have been compared, both on a term-by-term basis and over the entire degree program.

A total of 2,846 junior college students who transferred in 1960 received their degrees in 1962, or about 45 percent of those who had been granted junior standing at the time they transferred. This group was augmented by some 1,180 students who transferred before 1960 and who graduated in the spring of 1962, giving a total transfer comparison group of 4,026 graduates. The native group which received their degrees at the same time numbered 3,349. Nearly 700 native students who had expected to graduate in 1962 did not complete their requirements at that time and had to be dropped from the sample, with the result that the native and transfer comparison groups differed in size.

To recapitulate, the study dealt with a core group of 7,243 junior college students who entered four-year institutions in the fall of 1960, primarily as full-time students with junior standing; and with comparison groups of 4,026 transfer students (2,846 of whom transferred in 1960, 1,180 at an earlier date) and 3,349 native students who graduated in 1962.

Timing of the Study

A majority of the junior college students whose performance was studied entered some type of college in 1958 and persisted in continuous attendance until graduation or permanent withdrawal, including transfer in 1960 with no lapse in enrollment. The remainder entered college before 1958 and pursued various patterns of attendance. The core group of junior college students was identified in the spring of 1961, the graduate comparison groups in the spring of 1962. The first research grant was made for only a two-year longitudinal study, on the assumption that the group which was selected for study had a reasonable probability of graduating two years after transfer. Preliminary findings early in 1962 showed quite clearly that a majority of the 1960 group would not live up to the expectation of graduation in 1962. A second grant was then secured for a further follow-up which ended in the fall of 1963, at the beginning of the students' fourth year after transfer.

The major points of data collection were the spring of 1961, when a biographical questionnaire was administered to the transfer students and when preliminary performance data were obtained; the fall of 1961, when an enrollment check was made and dropout questionnaires were sent to the students who were no longer enrolled; the spring of 1962, when a biographical questionnaire was administered to the candidates for graduation in the native sample and to the additional transfer students; late summer of 1962, when complete transcripts were obtained for all native and transfer students; and the fall of 1963, when a final enrollment check was made. Test results were also obtained for large numbers of students who participated in various state and institutional testing programs, some of which were at the high school level, others at the point of freshman college admission, and still others at the time of transfer. A continuing follow-up was made of the students who dropped out, as new enrollment information became available.

Extensive field work was begun early in 1961 when arrangements were made for the identification of students and for data collection by the participating institutions. Field work ended with the close of the spring term in 1962. Interview data were obtained in a series of campus visits during the first six months of 1962, both from transfer students and from faculty and staff in each institution. In addition, the field work included participation in various statewide meetings at which problems of mutual concern to the two- and four-year colleges were discussed. These included meetings of registrars and admission officers, counselors and student personnel administrators, and academic deans.

Types of Data Analyzed

The two major types of data which were used in the various analyses are college transcripts and responses to the biographical questionnaire. Complete transcripts of work taken at the four-year colleges were obtained for all students. Junior college transcripts and forms showing the evaluation of junior college credit were also obtained for students whose four-year institutions gave only scant information about the junior college record on their own transcripts. The records of the four-year colleges showed all work through the 1962 summer session, unless the student graduated or withdrew before that time. An attempt was also made to obtain transcripts for students who dropped out and subsequently entered other four-year institutions, when the fact of their transfer could be established.

Extensive information relating to the nonacademic characteristics of the 1960 transfer students was obtained from the questionnaire which was administered during their spring term after transfer. Its ninety-nine items were drawn from four major areas: personal and family characteristics, decision-making about college and career, evaluation of junior college experiences and transfer problems, and participation in extracurricular activities. An abbreviated, twenty-item form of the questionnaire was administered to the samples of native students and the additional transfer students during the term in which they completed their degree requirements. Questionnaires were completed by 84 percent of the 1960 transfer students and by nearly 90 percent of the graduate comparison groups.

Transfer students who dropped out or were dismissed for poor scholarship were sent an additional questionnaire as soon as their status was made known by the college. They were requested to regard the questionnaire as a kind of substitute for a personal interview and to give whatever information they deemed appropriate to supplement their answers to the questions. Unlike the biographical questionnaires, the questions in the dropout instruments were unstructured and were not intended to yield data for formal statistical analysis. Two forms of the questionnaire were developed, one for students who withdrew voluntarily and a second for students who were dismissed. The questions in both were designed to elicit information about the circumstances leading to the student's withdrawal, the kind of help he sought and received while making a decision to withdraw or when he was confronted with dismissal, his current activities, and his plans to continue his education. Responses were obtained from only 36 percent of the dropouts—31 percent of those who were dismissed and 38 percent of those who withdrew voluntarily. Rather large numbers of the dropouts could not be located after they left the campus, particularly dropouts from institutions in large metropolitan areas. Some students who were classified as dropouts apparently declined to respond on the grounds that they transferred to another institution, rather than dropped out of college. Although post-dropout information was lacking for many students, biographical information was available for most and transcripts were obtained for all for use in various analyses.

Interviews were conducted with a sample of ten students on each campus during their fourth semester after transfer. Biographical and transcript information was used to select interviewees with

17

different academic and personal characteristics. The interviews were relatively unstructured and ranged over a broad spectrum of problems of adjustment to the four-year institution, satisfactions with and criticisms of the junior college, and suggestions for better articulation between the two types of colleges. Interviews were also held with selected staff members on each four-year college campus representing various areas of administration, student personnel, and instruction.

Finally, various types of material were collected for use in interpreting the findings relating to performance. These included catalogs, institutional studies, orientation materials, state statistics, and articulation conference proceedings.

Summary of Major Findings

Student Characteristics. Much of the variability in personal characteristics which was anticipated in the transfer student group simply was not found. As the junior college freshman class is almost indistinguishable from the high school graduating class, so is the junior college transfer group like the native student population found in the four-year colleges. The transfer students were mostly white, Protestant, of native-born parentage, and under twenty-one years of age when they entered the senior institutions. There were many more men than women in the transfer group. The high school record of the men was not as good as that of the women. However, a majority of both groups took a general or college preparatory program in high school and graduated in the upper half of their class.

Economic factors played a major role in the decisions of the transfer students to attend a two-year college as freshmen. The fathers of a large segment of the group worked in skilled or semi-skilled occupations which reflected the low level of formal education many had completed. The male students in particular could count on relatively little financial support from their parents, either in junior college or after transfer. For this reason they attended a junior college where tuition and fees were low and where it was possible for them to live at home with their parents, often while gainfully employed at the same time.

The transfer students tended to give somewhat negative reasons for choosing a junior college, but they gave high ratings to the quality of the education they had received. They praised both their junior college instructors and the scope of the curricular offerings. Junior college counseling and advising received higher ratings than did similar services offered by the four-year institutions, but the ratings were less favorable than those given to the various facets of instruction. On the whole, the transfer students were very well satisfied with their experience in junior college and encountered few serious problems in the four-year institutions.

Academic Performance. Sixty-two percent of the junior college students were granted their baccalaureate degrees within three years after transfer and 9 percent were still enrolled at the beginning of the fourth year. It is estimated that at least 75 percent of the group will receive their degrees eventually, including some dropouts who transferred to other institutions and others who planned to re-enter the same institution. While the eventual graduation rate will apparently be good, fewer than half the students graduated on time, i.e., at the end of two-plus-two or one-plus-three year programs. The record of the students who transferred with junior standing was much better than that of students who transferred with lower class standing, in terms of both persistence and on-time completion of program.

Most junior college students experienced some drop in grades when they transferred, particularly in their first term. The first-term differential was only -0.3 for the entire group, but there was a wide range of differentials among the various two- and four-year colleges. The performance of the dropouts was clearly inferior to that of the graduates, both in junior college and after transfer. Both groups sustained some drop in grades immediately after transfer, but the latter group showed steady improvement in the grades they earned in subsequent terms.

On the whole the transfer students had about the same probability of success in each of the broad major fields. However, their experience differed in the various four-year institutions and in different states. Although attrition in engineering was no greater than in other fields, engineering transfer students tended to take longer to complete their programs than students in other major fields. However, they did not require more time than native students in engineering at most institutions. More than half the graduates received their degrees in an applied field, primarily in business administration, engineering, and teacher education. Nearly two-thirds of the women and one-fourth of the men planned to enter the teaching field after receiving their degrees and credentials, many of them after taking at least one year of graduate work.

Comparisons with Native Students. A comparative analysis of transfer and native students who received their baccalaureate degrees in 1962, regardless of the date of their initial registration in a junior college or four-year institution, showed that both groups took about the same number of terms to complete their programs after entering the upper division. Furthermore, the total amount of degree credit used to satisfy baccalaureate degree requirements was about the same for both groups. The percentages of graduates who completed their programs in four semesters (or six quarters) after attaining upper division standing were also about equal although the junior college group made somewhat greater use of the summer session as they neared the end of their programs. The male graduates who went to junior college were a year older, on the average, than those who took all their work in one institution, but this difference in age had existed when the two groups entered the upper division.

Test results showed that although there was considerable overlap in the test scores of the native and transfer students, the graduates who began their work in a university as freshmen tended to have more academic aptitude and a greater readiness to undertake college work than those who entered a two-year college. At many universities the native student group also earned higher grade point averages in the upper division than their classmates who were transfer students. The grades of the native students were found to improve steadily as they progressed through their degree programs. Although the junior college grades of the transfer students were higher than the freshman and sophomore grades of the natives, the junior college students experienced a drop in grades after transfer which placed them at a disadvantage in the upper division. The pattern of native–transfer differences was less likely to occur in the teachers colleges than in the major state universities.

Individual Characteristics Related to Success. The junior college student most likely to succeed in a four-year institution was found to be one who performed well both in high school and in junior college. Junior college grades were more highly related to performance after transfer than was high school performance. However, a poor high school record, e.g., rank in the lowest quintile of the graduating class, often forbode academic difficulty after transfer unless the junior college record was considerably above average.

Although the grade point average of the dropouts was lower than those of the graduates and the persisting students, their mean test scores did not differ significantly at most institutions for which analyses of test data were made. The average score of the dropouts was often lower on a variety of aptitude and proficiency measures, but there was a great deal of overlap in the distributions of scores earned by the graduates, the students who were still enrolled, and the dropouts.

Transfer students who made an early decision to attend college experienced less attrition and were more likely to graduate on time than those who delayed their decision until graduation from high school. Time of decision to transfer to a particular four-year college was not found to be a factor in the prediction of success, provided the decision was made by the end of the freshman year in junior college. The relationship between age and performance after transfer was rather complex because of factors of motivation, attendance patterns after high school, and financial backing. The two subgroups with the highest probability of completing a degree program were found to be (a) the early decision-makers who progressed from high school to junior college to four-year institution with no break in enrollment, provided they made academically realistic decisions about college and major, and (b) adults who dropped out after high school (or early in college) in order to follow some non-collegiate endeavor, particularly if they attended junior college immediately prior to entering a four-year institution. Social class variables did not appear to be related to success after transfer in any consistent manner, except as students lacking adequate financial support after transfer were prone to drop out.

Attrition after Transfer. At the beginning of the fourth year after transfer, 29 percent of the students were no longer enrolled and had not graduated from the institutions to which they had transferred in 1960. Only one-third of the dropouts were dismissed because of their unsatisfactory grades, but two-thirds had averages below C when they withdrew. While post-attrition information was lacking for a large percentage of the dropouts, there was considerable evidence that many—including a sizeable number of dismissed students —entered other four-year institutions where they successfully pursued degree programs.

Economic factors played a major role in the attrition of the transfer students. Many had transferred without a satisfactory plan for meeting their expenses at the four-year institutions, while others had family illness or other unanticipated expenses which drained their income or savings. Economic and motivational factors were intertwined for still another group of dropouts who found opportunities for employment or business ventures more attractive than continued enrollment in their degree programs. Financial problems were mentioned by a larger percentage of the students who withdrew voluntarily, motivational problems by a larger percentage of the dismissed students. Some of the motivational problems were apparently present when the students graduated from high school, including a lack of clearly defined interests, values, career plans, and, most important of all, a realistic self-image.

Institutional and State Differences. Vast differences were found in the success of the transfer students in the forty-three participating colleges and universities, in the five types of institutions into which the forty-three were grouped, and in the ten states in which the study was conducted. A student's probability of success after transfer depended heavily upon his choice of four-year institution in the particular state in which he attended junior college, in relation to his previous academic record. Students whose junior college average was below 2.5 (C+) were somewhat unlikely to earn satisfactory grades in many of the major state universities. Students with minimally satisfactory grades in junior college were more likely to be successful in colleges which placed major emphasis on the preparation of teachers than in other types of institutions. However, there was wide variation in the findings for individual institutions and in the factors which produced institutional differences. A few of the factors were found to be the quality of the native students with whom the transfer students competed for grades, the size and complexity of the institution, and the institution's philosophy concerning undergraduate instruction and advisement.

Junior college transfer students were also found to have a higher probability of obtaining a baccalaureate degree in some states than in others, in spite of large differences among institutions. A few of the rather complex factors which appeared to produce state differences are these: the extent to which opportunity to transfer was restricted to students with above-average grades in junior college; the degree of diversification of curricular offerings in engineering, business administration, and other specialized fields in the various four-year colleges; and the development of good guidance and articulation programs involving the various levels of secondary and higher education.

Policies and Practices. Most students with at least a C average in their junior college program had a fairly wide range of four-year institutions to which they could transfer in 1960. By 1964 the open door to transfer admission had closed only slightly as a result of increased selectivity at the freshman level and limitations on enrollment in the preferred institutions. However, the prevailing philosophy continued to be one which advocated freedom for junior college students with a C average to transfer to the institution of their choice. At the same time, there had developed a greatly increased emphasis on guidance. There was also an increase in the testing of transfer students by 1964, but the expectation was that the scores would be used in advising students, rather than in denying admission to those with satisfactory junior college records.

The four-year institutions were found to be fairly liberal in evaluating junior college courses for transfer credit, up to an amount equal to about half the baccalaureate degree program. However, very few institutions credited the students with the grades they earned in junior college, either in applying retention standards or in determining eligibility for graduation. Furthermore, there was some trend toward disallowing courses in which grades of D were earned before transfer. On the whole, the trend was toward the liberalization of policies governing the evaluation of transfer credit, an example being the removal of all restriction on amount by some institutions and the substitution of an increased residence requirement.

Articulation and Coordination. The area in which the most significant changes occurred during the course of the study was that of articulation and coordination among the two- and four-year colleges. At the start of the study it was primarily the major state universities which were attempting to work with the junior colleges. Other four-year institutions limited their attention to high school relations. Formal coordination was also rather new at that time, at least as it is presently conceived. But by 1964 articulation had become the concern of all institutions which admitted sizeable numbers of transfer students. At the same time, in state after state, mechanisms for formal coordination among institutions were being built into master plans for higher education. Impetus for both articulation and coordination came from the increased demands for higher education, the expected bulge in college-age youth in the mid-1960's, and the financial problems faced by the various states in attempting to afford adequate educational opportunity for all beyond the high school.

3

Performance
of the Transfer Students

THE findings from the study of greatest interest to the colleges and universities which must make decisions about applicants for admission and to the high school graduates who must decide what type of college to attend are, of course, those relating to how well junior college transfer students perform. In fact, the most important single question which the study was designed to answer is believed to be: What is the probability that a student who begins his baccalaureate degree program in a two-year college will complete it if he transfers to a four-year institution? From this major focus of concern come questions involving the grade point achievement of the transfer students, the amounts of time and credit they need in order to complete their degree programs, comparisons with students who take all their work in a single four-year institution, and reasons why some transfer students fail to attain their degree objectives.

The first grant from the U.S. Office of Education was for a two-year follow-up study of junior college students who transferred with junior standing and who were classified as full-time students at a four-year institution. A check of the student records two full calendar years after they transferred, at the end of the 1962 summer session, showed that only 45 percent had graduated. The records also showed that at that time slightly more than half the nongraduates were still enrolled at the same college to which they had transferred in 1960—some after a break in attendance, but most in continuing status. Furthermore, many of the dropouts either were enrolled at another institution or expected to re-enroll at the college from which they had withdrawn. Because of the somewhat ambiguous nature of the findings that fewer than half the transfer students graduated on time, a third-year follow-up study was undertaken which included both the nongraduates who were still enrolled and the dropouts who entered other institutions.

Performance as Attainment of the Degree

After three full calendar years following transfer, 62 percent of the junior college students had been granted their baccalaureate degrees. (See Table 2.) Nine percent were still enrolled and expected to graduate within the next year. At least 4 percent had trans-

TABLE 2: ENROLLMENT STATUS OF THE JUNIOR COLLEGE STUDENTS
THREE YEARS AFTER TRANSFER
(In percent)

Sex	Enrollment Status				
	Graduated	Still Enrolled	Dropped Out		
			Voluntary	Dismissed	Total
Men	61	10	17	12	29
Women	64	4	24	8	32
Total	62	9	19	10	29

ferred to other institutions which granted them their undergraduate degrees or entered a graduate professional school before completing a degree program. Therefore, it is estimated that at least 75 percent and probably as high as 80 percent of the junior college transfer students achieved their degree objectives during the four-year period which began with their transfer to a four-year college or university in 1960.

Attrition among the students who transferred from junior colleges in 1960 was 29 percent. The figure seems rather high, considering that most of the students had already successfully completed two full years of college. However, the finding is tempered by the fact that only 10 percent of the transfer students (or about one-third of the dropouts) were required to withdraw because of unsatisfactory grades. Even among the 10 percent there were many who probably could have continued if they had petitioned for reinstatement under institutional policies which were then in effect.

While only one-third of the dropouts were dismissed for poor scholarship, another third were earning grade point averages below C when they withdrew. Some students in this latter group of dropouts would probably have been subject to dismissal if they had persisted longer. In some instances their grade point deficiencies were so great that it would have been almost impossible, both mathematically and academically, for them to achieve an over-all average of C during the remainder of their degree programs. Thus about 20 percent of the total transfer group dropped out after failing to perform at the minimally acceptable level required by the degree-granting institutions.

The probability of degree completion may then be answered from the present findings as follows: students who transfer from a two-year college with full junior standing have slightly less than two chances in three of completing their baccalaureate degree programs within a period of three years after transfer, if they enroll on a full-time basis. About two-thirds of those who complete degree programs do so within only two years after transfer with junior standing. The odds are about four chances in five that the students will complete a degree program eventually, with the time and institution unspecified. The probabilities are considerably lower for students who transfer with less than junior standing and for those who enroll on a part-time basis in a four-year institution.

Outcomes for Dropouts Who Enrolled Elsewhere

Information about dropouts who transferred to other colleges was obtained both from questionnaires sent to the students after their withdrawal and from transcripts. Since a rather poor return on the dropout questionnaire was secured, caution must be exercised in generalizing from the findings to the total dropout group. Among those who supplied information, 44 percent were enrolled in another institution at the time they filled out their questionnaire. One-third of the group of second-time transfers had been dismissed from the previous institution. A number of them re-entered junior college and others were admitted to smaller, less complex colleges than the ones in which they had earned poor grades. The dropouts who left voluntarily often transferred to institutions in their home communities or in metropolitan areas where they expected to obtain regular employment while completing their degree programs.

Good records were made by more than three-fourths of the dropouts whose enrollment in another four-year institution could be verified. Forty-five percent graduated during the study, and fewer than 5 percent of those who were still enrolled at the close of the study had averages below C. Only 5 percent were dismissed for poor scholarship. Graduation was delayed for many as a result of their break in enrollment after dropping out, changes in major, reduced course loads, and other factors associated with the move to another institution. The outcomes for dropouts who entered junior college or who enrolled in extension or other nonresident programs are not clear from the data. Enrollment in these programs did not lead directly to a baccalaureate degree, and time did not permit a sufficiently long follow-up of the students to find out how many were readmitted to (and successful in) resident degree programs. Some may have chosen terminal–vocational programs when they entered junior college for a second time or short-term courses in extension programs.

The dropouts who tranferred to other four-year institutions during the study were found to have good records of persistence with satisfactory grades and graduation. The data do not reflect the true incidence of transfer after dropout, but the findings are quite clear that some junior college students who experienced failure at first after transfer were later successful in other types of colleges and universities. Others undoubtedly could have succeeded if they had had guidance about other opportunities for transfer at the time of their withdrawal.

Grade Point Achievement

A widespread tendency was noted for the first-term grades of the transfer students to drop below their cumulative junior college averages. A differential of −0.3 was found for the entire group, but there was a very wide range of differentials for the various two- and four-year colleges. If the comparison had been made with grades earned in the last semester of junior college, the differential would have been much larger. The grades of most transfer students improved over the period of two years which they spent in junior college, declined in the first term after transfer, and then improved in successive terms, at least for those students who persisted to graduation.

The average semester grades for the total group increased from 2.27 (C+) for the first semester after transfer to 2.42 for the second, 2.54 for the third, and 2.68 for the fourth, for a total gain of 0.4. However, improvement beyond the second semester took place only in the grades of the graduates and the students who persisted to the end of the study. (See Table 3.) The mean grade point average of the graduates was 2.57 for the first term after transfer and 2.84 for the last. On the other hand, the group which was dismissed earned an average of only 1.33 for the first term after transfer and about 1.45 for each succeeding term, as the number of students in this category diminished with each wave of new dismissals. The record of the group which withdrew voluntarily was slightly better, with a cumu-

27

TABLE 3: Semester and Cumulative Grade Point Averages Earned at the Four-Year Institutions by Students Who Graduated, Were Still Enrolled, Withdrew, or Were Dismissed Two Years after Transfer*

Semester after Transfer†	Status at End of Study	Type of Four-Year Institution					All Institutions Combined
		1	2	3	4	5	
First	Graduated	2.56	2.57	2.58	2.53	2.70	2.57
	Still enrolled	2.24	2.23	2.28	2.39	2.36	2.27
	Withdrawn	1.97	2.26	2.11	2.20	1.57	2.05
	Dismissed	1.27	1.48	1.38	1.36	1.31	1.33
	Total	2.20	2.36	2.30	2.31	2.20	2.27
Second	Graduated	2.69	2.67	2.67	2.65	2.90	2.68
	Still enrolled	2.41	2.28	2.36	2.37	2.47	2.37
	Withdrawn	2.16	2.22	2.20	2.37	2.08	2.20
	Dismissed	1.45	1.43	1.49	1.57	1.87	1.47
	Total	2.41	2.45	2.42	2.42	2.54	2.42
Third	Graduated	2.75	2.78	2.72	2.73	2.89	2.75
	Still enrolled	2.42	2.33	2.37	2.36	2.47	2.39
	Withdrawn	1.96	2.30	2.04	2.15	1.63	2.04
	Dismissed	1.42	1.49	1.50	1.39	1.54	1.45
	Total	2.55	2.59	2.52	2.49	2.53	2.54
Fourth	Graduated	2.85	2.86	2.82	2.80	2.74	2.84
	Still enrolled	2.54	2.48	2.47	2.41	2.21	2.49
	Dismissed	1.66	1.35	1.21	1.58	1.38	1.46
	Total	2.71	2.70	2.66	2.59	2.42	2.68
Cumulative Grade Point Average	Graduated	2.71	2.73	2.70	2.68	2.81	2.71
	Still enrolled	2.37	2.31	2.37	2.38	2.41	2.36
	Withdrawn	1.87	2.20	2.06	2.22	1.49	1.99
	Dismissed	1.28	1.39	1.32	1.41	1.49	1.32
	Total	2.28	2.43	2.36	2.36	2.24	2.34

* Grade point average for the first two years after transfer (or until withdrawal, if it occurred before the end of the second year).

† The third quarter was equated to the second semester, the fourth quarter to the third semester, and the sixth quarter to the fourth semester. No enrollment check was made for the fifth semester, which accounts for the absence of a "Withdrawn" entry for the fourth semester.

lative upper division average of 1.99. The group's semester average hovered around 2.0 as new withdrawals occurred after each semester. Thus the total group increases in grade point average from term to term were the result of both improvement in the performance of the students who persisted and attrition among the poorer students. The assertion that students who drop out are just as capable as those who persist and graduate was found in this study to be false, although many good students did withdraw for various reasons.

Comparisons with Native Student Graduates[1]

Analysis of the records made by native and transfer students who were granted their baccalaureate degrees in 1962 revealed small but statistically significant differences between the two groups in the grades they earned at both the lower and upper division levels. (See Table 4.) However, the pattern of differences was reversed for the two levels. The junior college grades of the transfer students were often higher than the lower division grades of the natives, but the native students often earned higher grades than the transfer students in the upper division when the two groups were in direct competition for grades. The native students as a group bettered their own record as they moved through the lower division into the last two years, as they began to take a considerable amount of work in their major fields. The transfer graduates did not show the same steady pattern of improvement in grades because of the drop they experienced when they began their studies at the four-year institutions. About 30 percent of the transfer graduates earned averages below C for at least one term in the upper division, compared with only 20 percent of the native graduates.

The mean scores earned by the native and transfer students on various academic aptitude and achievement tests were examined at a number of institutions as a possible factor relating to the differences in the upper division grades earned by the two groups. Comparisons of graduates from five institutions involved test data obtained for both native and transfer students at the same time, e.g., in a twelfth-grade statewide testing program, while comparisons at four institutions involved test data obtained at different times, e.g., at the time each group entered the four-year institution. The findings were somewhat difficult to interpret because of the differences in the time of testing and the different tests used by the various institutions. However, the several statistical analyses all led to the general conclusion that graduates who began their degree work in the universities as freshmen had somewhat greater academic aptitude and ability than those who began their work in a two-year college.[2] Differences between the male comparison groups were significant in a larger number of the statistical tests made for various universities than differences between the groups of women.

[1] See pp. 61–3 for a comparison of the time and credit needed by the two groups to complete their degree programs.
[2] See Dorothy M. Knoell and Leland L. Medsker, *Articulation Between Two-Year and Four-Year Colleges* (Berkeley: Center for the Study of Higher Education, University of California, 1964), pp. 51–74, for detailed results of the significance tests.

TABLE 4: NATIVE-TRANSFER STUDENT COMPARISONS OF GRADE POINT AVERAGES,*
BY TYPE AND INDIVIDUAL INSTITUTIONS

A. Major State Universities (Type 1)

INSTITUTION	STUDENT COMPARISON GROUPS							
	Lower Division			Upper Division			First Term	
	Native	Junior College Transfer	P	Native	Transfer	P	Upper Division Native	After Transfer
University of California:								
Berkeley Campus	2.71	2.96	.01	2.88	2.66	.01	2.85	2.56
Los Angeles Campus	2.65	2.95	.01	2.85	2.67	.01	2.83	2.59
University of Florida	2.42	3.02	.01	2.84	2.73	n.s.	2.68	2.56
University of Georgia	2.55	2.67	n.s.	2.94	2.69	.01	2.77	2.48
University of Illinois	2.72	2.96	.01	2.93	2.80	n.s.	2.91	2.63
University of Kansas	2.69	2.94	.01	2.85	2.60	.01	2.74	2.62
University of Michigan	2.71	3.06	.01	2.88	2.68	.01	2.79	2.58
Pennsylvania State University	2.53	2.52	n.s.	2.77	2.60	.01	2.64	2.36
University of Texas	2.70	3.09	.01	2.90	2.68	.01	2.87	2.64
University of Washington	2.69	2.96	.01	2.92	2.73	.01	2.84	2.60
Total	2.64	2.92	.01	2.88	2.68	.01	2.79	2.56

*All grades have been converted to C=2. Significance levels for the statistical tests of differences in the means are given in the column to the right of various pairs of means.

30

TABLE 4—*Continued*
B. Teachers College (Type 2)

INSTITUTION	STUDENT COMPARISON GROUPS							
	Lower Division			Upper Division			First Term	
	Native	Junior College Transfer	P	Native	Transfer	P	Upper Division Native	After Transfer
Georgia Southern College	3.06	2.62	.01	3.06	2.67	.01	2.87	2.58
Kansas State College of Pittsburg	2.54	2.83	.01	2.75	2.79	n.s.	2.73	2.62
Kansas State Teachers College of Emporia	2.57	2.70	n.s.	2.72	2.67	n.s.	2.58	2.46
Central Michigan University	2.46	2.62	.05	2.79	2.61	.02	2.66	2.40
Eastern Michigan University	2.50	2.46	n.s.	2.70	2.72	n.s.	2.70	2.77
Western Michigan University	2.66	2.54	.05	2.94	2.80	.02	2.81	2.66
State University of New York:								
College at New Paltz	2.63	2.68	n.s.	2.63	2.79	.05	2.69	2.77
College at Oswego	2.43	2.54	n.s.	2.66	2.57	.02	2.50	2.44
Sam Houston State Teachers College	2.53	2.64	n.s.	2.64	2.68	n.s.	2.55	2.45
Western Washington State College	2.66	2.59	n.s.	2.90	2.65	.01	2.83	2.58
Total	2.60	2.62	n.s.	2.78	2.70	.01	2.69	2.56

31

TABLE 4—*Continued*

C. Other State Institutions (Type 3)

STUDENT COMPARISON GROUPS

INSTITUTION	Lower Division			Upper Division			First Term	
	Native	Junior College Transfer	P	Native	Transfer	P	Upper Division Native	After Transfer
Long Beach State College	2.55	2.61	n.s.	2.78	2.61	.01	2.71	2.52
San Francisco State College	2.51	2.60	n.s.	2.78	2.66	.01	2.72	2.61
Florida State University	2.39	2.69	.01	2.78	2.73	n.s.	2.59	2.53
Northern Illinois University	2.41	2.67	.01	2.58	2.55	n.s.	2.56	2.45
Southern Illinois University	2.65	2.62	n.s.	2.98	2.73	.02	2.79	2.64
Kansas State University	2.54	2.94	.01	2.77	2.59	.05	2.62	2.33
Michigan State University	2.65	2.61	n.s.	2.75	2.58	.01	2.68	2.46
Wayne State University	2.63	2.52	n.s.	2.92	2.76	.01	2.81	2.69
Texas Technological College	2.52	3.07	.01	2.83	2.69	.05	2.70	2.59
Washington State University	2.68	2.85	.05	2.84	2.69	.02	2.74	2.71
Total	2.54	2.73	.01	2.80	2.67	.01	2.69	2.57

TABLE 4—Continued

D. Private Universities (Type 4) and Technical Institutions (Type 5)

| | STUDENT COMPARISON GROUPS | | | | | | | |
| INSTITUTION | Lower Division | | | Upper Division | | | First Term | |
	Native	Junior College Transfer	P	Native	Transfer	P	Upper Division Native	After Transfer
Private Universities								
University of the Pacific	2.68	2.77	n.s.	2.89	2.83	n.s.	2.81	2.65
University of Southern California	2.69	—	—	2.98	2.71	.01	2.89	2.58
University of Miami	2.39	2.92	.01	2.84	2.88	n.s.	2.80	2.50
Emory University	2.46	2.87	.01	2.76	2.65	n.s.	2.64	2.46
Loyola University (Illinois)	2.61	2.83	n.s.	2.83	2.64	n.s.	2.62	2.44
Roosevelt University	2.75	2.54	n.s.	2.77	2.45	n.s.	2.82	2.35
Total	2.56	2.74	.01	2.83	2.68	.01	2.77	2.51
Technical Institutions								
Georgia Institute of Technology	2.34	3.42	.01	2.76	2.43	.02	2.71	2.30
Rochester Institute of Technology	2.71	2.87	n.s.	2.66	2.67	n.s.	2.68	2.74
Texas A&M University	2.42	2.82	.01	2.75	2.85	n.s.	2.61	2.72
Total	2.52	2.98	.01	2.71	2.67	n.s.	2.67	2.63

33

Comparisons were also made of the ability of the groups that graduated from one teachers college in the study. In this instance the conclusion was drawn that the native and transfer graduates probably did not differ in academic ability.

Differences in ability or readiness for college work thus appear to be useful as explanatory factors in the analysis of differences in grades earned at the upper division level in the various universities. Native student groups which were judged to have greater ability earned higher grades in the upper division although the lower division grades of the junior college students were often higher than those of the native students. At most universities the higher ability of the native graduates made it appear unreasonable to expect that the transfer students would be able to compete on a par with natives for upper division grades since the transfers had to make both an academic and a personal adjustment at the four-year institution.

Still another analysis showed that transfer students with very high ability, i.e., in the upper quintile, did not experience a serious handicap in competing with native students for grades which would qualify them for admission to graduate school. A few high ability transfer students suffered a considerable drop in grades after transfer, but most earned grades which were about as high as those of the native students with similar ability.

Factors Affecting Transfer Student Performance

Although the junior college performs an important salvage function for many high school graduates who are not equipped to enter a four-year college as freshmen, the findings from the study are quite clear that good junior college and post-transfer records are made primarily by students with good high school records, i.e., those who ranked in the upper half of their class or better. Sex differences, major fields, academic aptitude, transfer class standing, and socioeconomic characteristics were examined in some depth in an attempt to account for differences in performance on the part of individual students, regardless of the type of four-year college they were attending or the state in which the institution was located.

Sex Differences in Performance. The percentages of women who graduated two and three years after transferring from junior college were somewhat higher than those obtained for the men. However, attrition among the women by the end of the third year was also a little higher, with the net result that the eventual graduation record of the men was probably slightly better than that of the women. (See Table 2.) The most striking difference between the men and women was in the percentages of voluntary and forced withdrawals. The women tended to withdraw largely for personal reasons, with good grades, while a large percentage of the men were dismissed from the four-year colleges with poor grades. More than 40 percent of the men who dropped out were dismissed, compared with only one-fourth of the women.

The women also had a greater tendency to graduate "on time," two years after transfer as juniors. The percentage of on-time graduates among the women was 55, compared with only 42 percent of the men. Some of the men who were delayed were in engineering programs requiring more than two full years after transfer. Others took reduced course loads or attended somewhat sporadically after their first term. The men and women at what have been called the "other state institutions" differed greatly with respect to incidence of on-time graduation. Sixty percent of the women received their degrees from these institutions within two years after transfer, compared with only 41 percent of the men. However, by the end of the third year the difference in the percentage of men and women who graduated was considerably reduced as a result of the large number of male graduates in the third year.

Sex differences in outcomes at various points in the follow-up study appeared to be related to differences in choice of major, as well as to academic and personal factors. Women in teacher education programs had a high probability of graduating on time from most colleges because of both curricular and ability factors. Men who enrolled in engineering programs, on the other hand, had a rather low probability of graduating two years after transfer because of the large amount of credit which had to be earned in the upper division. Although most college catalogs represented the programs as four-year curricula, the course and credit requirements almost always exceeded those of liberal arts and other programs by at least the equivalent of one full term.

Factors which produced sex differences in success after transfer are thus somewhat difficult to isolate because of the differing choices of major by the men and women. The superior high school and junior college performance of the women was in part responsible for their lower rate of academic dismissal after transfer, but factors of major and college attended were also believed to play a part in determining performance outcomes.

Academic Aptitude. Aptitude and ability test data were analyzed for junior college students who transferred to ten four-year institutions located in six states, in order to find out the extent to which ability factors were related to success after transfer. A considerable amount of testing of both freshmen and transfer students is now being carried on by the various institutions, but little has been done with the results obtained for the transfer students. There is reason to believe that testing will assume a more important role in the future in the admission, evaluation, and placement of transfer students, particularly as admission at the freshman level becomes much more selective. The recent establishment of a Council on Examinations of Collegiate Achievement by the College Entrance Examination Board is but one indicator of a greatly increased interest in the use of standardized tests as students progress through college.

The analysis of test data in the transfer study was designed primarily to find out whether test results of various types might have been useful in identifying potential failures in the 1960 transfer group. Enrollment status two years after transfer was selected as the dependent variable for analysis, rather than grade point average. Analysis of variance tests were made of the differences in means earned by the groups of men and women at each college who graduated, dropped out, and were still enrolled two years after transfer. Some of the test data had been obtained in twelfth-grade testing programs, some in freshman admission programs, and some at the time of transfer. Various types of tests were included in the different programs, including academic aptitude, skill or proficiency, and subject-matter achievement. A total of ninety-six analyses of variance tests were made, only sixteen of which produced values of F which were significant at the .05 level or better. The mean scores of the dropouts tended to be lower than those of the other groups, but the overlap in the scores of the graduates, delayed graduates, and dropouts was very large, particularly in the groups of women.

The findings seem to suggest that the variance in the test scores of the junior college students is related to their success in four-year institutions if little or no selection has taken place on the basis of junior college achievement. But good counseling and screening tend to diminish the usefulness of test results in predicting achievement.

Significant differences among groups were found for four institutions in two states, apparently under quite different sets of circumstances. In one state the junior college grades of the students who transferred to the major state universities were no higher than those who transferred to the teachers colleges. Attrition among transfer students was high in each instance. Nonselective admission was both the practice and the philosophy of the state at that time. Entering transfers were quite heterogeneous with respect to both prior achievement and academic ability. The best students usually graduated, the poorest dropped out, and the difference in the ability of the two groups was very large.

In the second state the total score on a twelfth-grade test battery has been used by the state universities to screen freshman applicants for admission but has been largely ignored in the admission of transfer students. While the total score on the battery did not distinguish between successes and failures in the transfer group, the total score on the American Council on Education aptitude test did so for the male groups at both universities. It appears that some men with very low aptitude completed junior college programs but did not have the ability to succeed in some fields at the universities.

On the whole the findings from the analyses of test data seem to show that most four-year institutions could accommodate students with a rather wide range of academic ability because of the differing intellectual demands of the various majors offered. Furthermore, junior college grades alone appear to provide sufficient evidence of the students' ability to succeed in upper division work in particular institutions and in selected majors.[3]

Class Level at Time of Transfer. Both grade point achievement and amount of credit earned in junior college were found to be important factors in the success of the students after transfer. Students who transferred below the junior level are under-represented in the study because they were not included in the original design. However, the findings concerning their performance contrast quite vividly with those for students who transferred with full junior standing. Attrition in the group which was granted only sophomore standing was 45 percent, compared with only 26 percent in the group of junior level transfers. Furthermore, only 35 percent of the sophomores graduated within three years after transfer. Since only 20 percent of the group was still enrolled and expected to graduate during the fourth year after transfer, the total percentage of graduates was probably no more than 55, compared with at least 75 percent of the students who completed two years in junior college. The performance of the students who stayed in junior college for two years but who lost considerable credit in transferring was somewhat better than that of the sophomore group in terms of their rate of graduation but almost as poor with respect to attrition with poor grades. Nineteen percent of the group which lost credit was dismissed for poor scholarship, compared with 15 percent of the group which transferred with sophomore standing and only 9 percent of the group with full junior standing.

One of the major reasons for reduction of credit, and thus in class standing, at the time of transfer was unsatisfactory grades in some junior college courses. Therefore, it was not surprising to find that what might be called the sub-junior group did not perform as well

[3] See *Ibid.*, pp. 33–50, for further details on testing.

after transfer as their classmates who were granted upper division standing. However, the transfer students who had only one year in junior college were fairly good students before transfer and should have made a better record at the four-year institutions. The finding that only 35 percent graduated three years after transfer raises the question of the effectiveness of the junior college in preparing students who stay for only one year, if they require four more years to complete what is normally regarded as a four-year degree program. Analysis of the amount of transfer credit which these students received showed that many had earned somewhat more than enough for sophomore standing but not a sufficient amount to achieve a higher class standing. In spite of this unit advantage which the sophomore transfer group enjoyed, the percentage of students who earned degrees after one-plus-three years was considerably less than the percentage who earned degrees after two-plus-two years of college. Further research is needed which would focus on the students who spend only one year in junior college. However, the present data, while limited in volume, show very clearly the superiority of the performance of the group which transferred as juniors, whether as a result of better preparation in junior college, more adequate screening before transfer, or enrollment in courses in their major field after transfer at the junior level.

Junior College Grades. About two-thirds of the transfer students earned junior college averages below 2.6 (B—), about one-third below 2.4. About 6 percent transferred with cumulative averages below C. Many of this group had shown considerable improvement during their two years in junior college, yet nearly half dropped out a short time later, most of them with poor or failing grades. (See Table 5.) Students with junior college averages between 2.0 and 2.3 were somewhat more successful, with a total attrition rate of slightly more than one-third (including 27 percent who withdrew with poor or failing grades). As junior college averages increased above 2.3, attrition decreased accordingly. Attrition was only 28 percent for those with junior college averages between 2.4 and 2.7, 21 percent for those between 2.8 and 3.1, 18 percent for those between 3.2 and 3.5, and 12 percent for the small group above 3.5. Percentages of students who graduated on time also rose with increases in the junior college average. Only 31 percent of those with averages between 2.0 and 2.3 graduated two years after transfer, compared with nearly 60 percent of those with averages of 3.2 and higher.

The success of the transfer students with particular grade point averages in junior college depended heavily upon their choice of

TABLE 5: Enrollment Status Two Years after Transfer, by Junior College Grade Point Average and Type of Four-Year Institution

Junior College GPA	Enrollment Status	Type of Four-Year Institution										All Institutions Combined	
		1		2		3		4		5			
		Students	Percent	Students	Percent	Students	Percent	Students	Percent	Students	Percent	Students	Percent
3.6–4.0	Graduated		58		79		63		60		(2)*		61
	Still enrolled		31		13		24		13		(3)		27
	Withdrew with C		9		8		10		27		(2)		10
	Withdrew below C or dismissed		2		0		2		0		(1)		2
	Total	219		38		85		15		8		365	
3.2–3.5	Graduated		56		74		57		45		25		56
	Still enrolled		27		9		28		29		54		26
	Withdrew with C		11		17		11		22		7		12
	Withdrew below C or dismissed		7		0		4		3		14		6
	Total	437		84		181		58		28		788	
2.8–3.1	Graduated		42		64		55		39		27		47
	Still enrolled		33		21		30		33		50		31
	Withdrew with C		12		11		10		18		2		11
	Withdrew below C or dismissed		13		3		5		9		23		10
	Total	713		191		372		66		48		1,390	
2.4–2.7	Graduated		34		62		42		33		14		39
	Still enrolled		32		25		33		41		47		32
	Withdrew with C		9		8		11		19		3		10
	Withdrew below C or dismissed		24		4		15		7		36		18
	Total	950		276		605		105		59		1,995	
2.0–2.3	Graduated		24		40		34		19		23		31
	Still enrolled		33		32		35		37		48		34
	Withdrew with C		8		8		7		14		4		8
	Withdrew below C or dismissed		35		19		24		30		25		27
	Total	582		372		809		144		44		1,951	
Below 2.0	Graduated		21		20		23		14		(1)		20
	Still enrolled		20		44		34		24		(7)		32
	Withdrew with C		10		7		10		8		(1)		9
	Withdrew below C or dismissed		49		29		33		54		(3)		39
	Total	137		135		119		50		12		453	

* Figures in parentheses represent numbers of students, rather than percentages, and are used in place of percentages when the N for subgroups is less than 15.

four-year institution. Among the nearly two thousand students in the 2.0 to 2.3 range of junior college grades, 35 percent of those who transferred to the major state universities withdrew with poor grades, compared with only 19 percent of those who entered teachers colleges. If the group which transferred to the Pennsylvania State University were omitted from the computations, attrition would be much higher than 35 percent. Attrition at the other types of colleges among students with this range in averages was found to be 24 percent for the other state universities, 25 percent for the technical institutions, and 30 percent for the private universities.

A very clear implication from the findings is that a junior college average of only C should not be regarded as adequate and sufficient evidence of a student's ability to do satisfactory work at the upper division level at all institutions, even in the public sector of higher education, nor in all major fields. However, at present there appears to be at least one public four-year institution in each state where junior college students with C averages have a fair chance of achieving their degree objectives. At the same time the number of universities where this is true is decreasing rapidly, particularly for students who enroll in engineering and business administration programs. The private universities differed very widely in how well they were able to accommodate transfer students with C averages. Some would not admit such students, others admitted them but dropped them soon afterward with poor grades, and still others were successful with C students.

Other Personal Characteristics. Most nonacademic characteristics were found to have much less relationship to student performance than was found for high school and junior college achievement. Significant relationships were found for some samples of men and women at different types of colleges when enrollment outcomes were related to family nationality, parents' educational attainment, and father's occupation. The findings tended to support the belief that students with lower class backgrounds who persisted through junior college and transferred would be just as likely to succeed as those with middle and upper class backgrounds who had had fewer handicaps to overcome. Neither age nor attendance pattern by itself was related to success after transfer. However, the best over-all record was made by the young students who moved directly from high school to junior college, who stayed in junior college for two full years, and who transferred without a break to a four-year institution.

Good records were also made by students who attended two and sometimes several different colleges before transfer in 1960. Students who were considerably older than the junior college average had a high rate of persistence and were quite likely to graduate on time. The poorest performance record was made by what are often regarded as the "late bloomers," i.e., males with poor high school records who earn C grades in junior college which are high enough to transfer but poor indicators of ability to do further college work. Another group which experienced difficulty after transfer was the students who worked at full-time jobs while attending junior college, often taking three or four years to complete the lower division program.

No single variable was found to be useful in predicting success for all students, in all majors, and across all institutions and states. The importance of good counseling seems clear. With the current advances in knowledge about factors affecting performance, a more effective matching of junior college student and transfer institution should soon be within reach.

Student Views of Their Performance

The transfer students were queried about grading standards both in a questionnaire which was administered in the spring term after transfer and in interviews conducted a year later. They were asked to make comparisons of grading in the two- and four-year colleges and to evaluate their own grade-getting ability after transfer. Only 20 percent of the students said that differences in grading standards in the two types of colleges were more than a minor problem to them. A somewhat larger percentage said that an increase in the expectations of their instructors in both the quality and the quantity of work they had to do in order to receive satisfactory grades was a problem for them.

In interviews the transfer students had few complaints about the fairness of the grading in the four-year colleges. However, many complained about the loss of their junior college grade points when they transferred. On many campuses the students believed that their good junior college grades were all reduced to C's by the four-year colleges; actually, most institutions simply ignored the junior college grades after admitting the transfer students, thus starting their upper division work with a zero grade point balance. The students recognized the right of the four-year institutions to insist upon their achieving a C average after transfer in order to qualify for a degree, but they resented having their junior college grades omitted from their new permanent records. They also said that they thought the faculty members in the four-year colleges were fair in assigning grades but, at the same time, they felt somewhat unprepared for the types of examinations and other evaluations given in the senior institutions.

A significant number of interviewees mentioned the problem of the meaning or value of a junior college grade of C. They felt that A and B grades in junior college were "earned" grades but that C grades were given for compliance as often as for satisfactory achievement. Compliance in this instance meant regular attendance in class, handing in assigned work on time, neatly typed papers, and generally proper classroom behavior. The students wished their junior college instructors might have expected more of them, in order that they might have been prepared for the more exacting standards of the four-year institutions. Some reported that they had been permitted (or even counseled) to enroll for an excessive number of courses each semester in junior college for which they received passing grades but in which they failed to learn all that they should have in order to go on in particular fields.

The student data seem to minimize the seriousness of grading problems in the four-year institutions while pointing up some possible problems in junior college grading. The responses tend to confirm the findings concerning performance after transfer, notably that a C average in junior college does not insure success in all types of four-year institutions.

Problematic Practices Involving Grades

The junior college grade point average which is computed for use in admitting transfer students is generally regarded as a kind of global indicator of success after transfer, based on all work attempted in the junior college. In practice, many different averages are being computed by different four-year colleges from the same sets of grades. Naturally, different admissions decisions may result. Failure to charge students for courses which they repeated, dropped with failing grades, or did not complete in junior college produces an unrealistic average, particularly for borderline students. If these students had been "charged" for all units, and if other students had been evaluated more stringently who had excessive amounts of activity credit, many would have been refused admission who were later dismissed for poor grades. Inadequacies or lack of uniformity in the junior college transcripts contributed to the problem of calculating a valid junior college average for admitting transfer students. Grade point requirements for junior college graduation are often stated in different terms from those for transfer admission, e.g., as some minimum number of units completed with a C average, rather than a C average on all units attempted. Since a very large percentage of students transfer with only a C average, random variation in methods of computing transfer averages has an important effect on the evaluation of performance.

Still another problem is what minimum passing grades should be accepted in awarding transfer credit for particular courses, when the over-all average is at least C. While present practice still leans toward the acceptance of D grades, there is some trend toward discounting D grades in awarding unit credit. Although students would not be required to repeat courses in which D grades were earned in junior college, unless doing so was clearly to their advantage in undertaking further work in the field, they would be required to take other courses in their place. As grading standards increase and competition becomes tougher, the conditions under which D grades are accepted for both course and unit credit need to be examined more carefully.

Finally, the use of junior college grades after an admissions decision has been made is problematic. It now seems quite apparent that the four-year colleges will require at least a C average on all work after transfer as a condition for granting the degree. Thus earlier grades would have no bearing on eligibility for graduation. However, the use of junior college grades in deciding whether to place a student on academic probation and then to dismiss him is less clear-cut. Practice tends toward disregarding junior college grades after admission under all circumstances. A transfer student who falls below C at the end of his first semester is thus automatically placed on probation. If he fails to make up his deficiency at the end of the next term, he is often subject to dismissal without regard to his junior college record. Practice would seem less unfair if retention policies (and the results of their application) were considered in setting admission standards for transfer students. Many institutions are admitting students who have very little probability of being able to succeed, when the institution's differential with junior college grades is related to its retention standards.

4

State and Institutional
Differences in Performance

THE success of the junior college in performing the transfer function is dependent not only on the quality of its students and the lower division preparation it offers them, but also on the effectiveness with which it assists transfer students in selecting four-year institutions and programs in which they have a reasonable probability of doing satisfactory work. In 1960 the admission policies for transfer students from junior colleges might be characterized as "open door" in most of the states which participated in the study, in the sense that any student who earned at least a C average in his junior college work was eligible to transfer at will to most public four-year institutions and to a considerable number of private ones. Furthermore, many students with slightly less than a C average in junior college could also gain admittance to one or several institutions if they showed promise of improvement or earned satisfactory test scores, or if they could demonstrate some other compensating characteristics. The major exceptions to this open-door approach to transfer admission were the University of California and University of Michigan, among the public institutions, and certain private universities which reserved the right to select their students whether or not they were in actuality highly selective.

Few institutions reviewed the high school records of their transfer applicants, on the grounds that all high school graduates were admissible as freshmen. The University of California differed in this regard by requiring applicants who were not eligible for freshman admission to earn a grade point average of C+ (2.4) and to complete at least fifty-six units of college work before transfer. The University of Michigan has been selective over a long period of time insofar as an individual decision is made about each applicant for admission with advanced standing, taking into account his high school and college records, the quality of the performance of previous transfer students from his junior college, and the probability of his being able to do satisfactory work in his choice of major. The university expects most applicants to present junior college averages of about 2.5 in order to have some cushion for the drop in grades which is anticipated immediately after transfer.

As the four-year colleges become more selective at the freshman level, they are also becoming aware of the necessity for examining their policies for admitting transfer students along at least two lines:

1. When should a junior college student be permitted to transfer to a four-year college if he was not eligible for freshman admission? after one semester? one year? after receiving his associate in arts degree? or not at all?

2. What grade point average should the junior college transfer student be required to earn if the four-year college is selective at the freshman level? Should the required average be tied to the grade point differential between the junior college and first-term grades after transfer? to a probability level of success after transfer? to native student performance?

Diversity in the Four-Year Institutions

Performance of transfer students varied considerably by types of institutions to which they transferred, and among individual institutions. (See Tables 6 and 7.) As was expected, transfer students in the ten teachers colleges achieved the highest rate of graduation (73 percent) and the lowest rate of attrition (21 percent). The poorest performance record was earned by the students who transferred to the three technical institutions and to the eight private universities. Only slightly more than half the junior college students graduated within three years after transfer to these types of institutions, and attrition was about one-third. Variation among the institutions was very large, however. The range in percentages of graduates from the private universities was from 32 to 80. In the technical institutions the percentages of graduates at the end of the study were found to be 29, 46, and 72. The two types of state universities had graduation rates of about 62 percent and attrition rates of about 30 percent, which fell midway between the rates for the other types of institutions. Somewhat less variation in graduation and attrition rates

45

TABLE 6: Enrollment Status of the Junior College Students
Three Years after Transfer, by Type of
Four-Year Institution

Type of Four-Year Institution	Sex	Enrollment Status (In percent)				
		Graduated	Still Enrolled	Dropped Out		
				Voluntary	Dismissed	Total
1	Men	60	10	16	14	30
	Women	60	3	26	11	37
	Total	60	8	19	13	32
2	Men	73	8	12	7	19
	Women	73	3	18	6	24
	Total	73	6	14	7	21
3	Men	62	10	17	11	28
	Women	68	5	23	4	27
	Total	64	8	19	9	28
4	Men	56	12	21	11	32
	Women	48	9	36	7	43
	Total	53	11	26	10	36
5	Total	51	16	30	3	33
All institutions	Men	61	10	17	12	29
	Women	64	4	24	8	32
	Total	62	9	19	10	29

was found among the state universities than was found among the private universities and technical institutions.

An example of rather extreme differences between types is found in the incidence of dismissal. At the major state universities 41 percent of the dropouts were dismissed for poor scholarship, but only 11 percent of the dropouts from the technical institutions were required to withdraw. The difference is related at least in part to the varying policies of the institutions concerned. The major state universities tended to dismiss any student whose grade point average was less than C at the end of the first year after transfer, while the technical institutions were more inclined to permit students with unsatisfactory grades to continue beyond the first year. However, voluntary attrition was high at the latter type of institution among

TABLE 7: ENROLLMENT STATUS OF THE JUNIOR COLLEGE STUDENTS THREE YEARS AFTER TRANSFER, BY TYPE AND INDIVIDUAL INSTITUTIONS (In percent)

A. Major State Universities (Type 1)

INSTITUTION	GRADUATED			STILL ENROLLED			WITHDRAWN		
	Men	Wom-en	Total	Men	Wom-en	Total	Men	Wom-en	Total
University of California:									
Berkeley Campus	60	59	60	9	2	7	31	39	33
Los Angeles Campus	72	60	68	7	2	5	21	38	27
University of Florida	56	54	56	11	6	10	32	40	34
University of Georgia	71	71	71	5	2	5	24	27	24
University of Illinois	39	59	43	9	2	8	52	39	49
University of Kansas	44	66	50	12	2	10	44	32	40
University of Michigan	50	71	57	23	4	17	27	25	26
Pennsylvania State University	71	76	72	11	2	9	18	22	19
University of Texas	60	54	58	11	3	9	29	43	33
University of Washington	50	44	49	14	5	12	36	51	39
Total	60	60	60	10	3	8	30	37	32

B. Teachers Colleges (Type 2)

INSTITUTION	GRADUATED			STILL ENROLLED			WITHDRAWN		
	Men	Wom-en	Total	Men	Wom-en	Total	Men	Wom-en	Total
Georgia Southern College	90	92	91	2	0	1	8	8	8
Kansas State College of Pittsburg	62	74	66	5	3	4	33	23	30
Kansas State Teachers College of Emporia	87	76	83	3	0	2	10	24	15
Central Michigan University	60	79	68	14	0	8	26	21	24
Eastern Michigan University	79	75	77	7	7	7	14	18	16
Western Michigan University	72	77	74	12	4	9	16	19	17
State University of New York:									
College at New Paltz	69	38	50	8	0	3	23	62	47
College at Oswego	85	83	85	2	0	2	12	17	13
Sam Houston State Teachers College	77	68	74	11	3	9	12	29	17
Western Washington State College	72	55	67	8	5	8	20	40	25
Total	73	73	73	8	3	6	19	24	21

C. Other State Institutions (Type 3)

INSTITUTION	GRADUATED			STILL ENROLLED			WITHDRAWN		
	Men	Wom-en	Total	Men	Wom-en	Total	Men	Wom-en	Total
Long Beach State College	62	73	67	11	7	9	27	20	24
San Francisco State College	51	52	51	11	5	9	38	43	40
Florida State University	81	78	80	1	5	2	18	17	18
Northern Illinois University	73	72	73	2	0	2	25	28	25
Southern Illinois University	76	67	73	9	11	10	14	22	17
Kansas State University	50	50	50	15	11	14	35	39	36
University of Michigan:									
Dearborn Campus	58	75	61	19	8	17	23	17	22
Flint Campus	79	84	81	3	0	2	18	16	17
Michigan State University	77	78	77	4	4	4	18	18	19
Wayne State University	63	86	71	16	2	11	21	12	18
Texas Technological College	55	86	64	15	5	12	31	9	24
Washington State University	73	62	70	5	0	4	22	38	26
Total	62	68	64	10	5	8	28	27	28

47

TABLE 7—*Continued*

D. Private Universities (Type 4) and Technical Institutions (Type 5)

INSTITUTION	GRADUATED			STILL ENROLLED			WITHDRAWN		
	Men	Women	Total	Men	Women	Total	Men	Women	Total
Private universities									
University of the Pacific	47	50	48	23	4	16	30	46	36
University of Southern California	82	74	80	9	6	8	9	20	11
University of Miami	44	25	37	7	19	12	48	56	51
Emory University	62	89	67	0	0	0	38	11	33
Loyola University (Illinois)	44	45	44	16	9	15	40	46	41
Roosevelt University	47	47	47	14	18	15	39	35	38
New York University	33	41	37	18	4	11	49	55	52
Seattle University	29	40	32	18	0	14	53	60	54
Total	56	48	53	12	9	11	32	43	36
Technical institutions									
Georgia Institute of Technology	—	—	29	—	—	25	—	—	45
Rochester Institute of Technology	—	—	46	—	—	14	—	—	40
Texas A&M University	—	—	72	—	—	12	—	—	16
Total	—	—	51	—	—	16	—	—	33

poor students who realized the unlikelihood of their ever being able to achieve the grade point average required for graduation.

Only the technical institutions enrolled a substantial portion of their students for a fourth undergraduate year after transfer. Most of the students who were thus delayed were enrolled in engineering programs with high unit requirements. If degrees were granted in due time to all who were still enrolled at the end of the study, the success rate for the technical institutions would reach 67 percent, which compares quite favorably with the 71 percent achieved by the total group of forty-three institutions.

Grade Point Achievement. Differences in the grades earned by the junior college students who transferred to the different types of four-year institutions appear at first glance to follow no meaningful pattern. (See Table 8.) The junior college grades of the students who transferred to the major state universities and technical institutions were higher than those of the students who entered other types of institutions, but their upper division grades earned after transfer were lower than those of the other students. Transfers to the teachers colleges had lower junior college grades, but earned among the highest upper division grades. There was a fairly close correspondence between rankings of the five types of institutions on the basis of (1) the upper division grades earned by the transfer students and (2) the percentages of transfer students who were granted the baccalaureate degree.

Several factors are believed to account for the observed

48

TABLE 8: Grade Point Averages Earned in Junior College and After Transfer and Grade Point Differentials, by Type and Individual Institutions

INSTITUTIONS BY TYPE	GRADE POINT AVERAGE* Junior College	Means Four-Year College First-term	Means Four-Year College Cumulative	Junior College Differentials First-term	Junior College Differentials Cumulative
Major State Universities					
University of California:					
Berkeley Campus	2.88	2.23	2.31	− .65	− .57
Los Angeles Campus	2.88	2.33	2.41	− .55	− .47
University of Florida	2.74	2.16	2.27	− .58	− .47
University of Georgia	2.66	2.10	2.29	− .56	− .37
University of Illinois	2.72	2.03	2.15	− .69	− .57
University of Kansas	2.65	1.96	2.01	− .69	− .64
University of Michigan	2.92	2.31	2.40	− .61	− .52
Pennsylvania State University	2.38	2.06	2.29	− .32	− .09
University of Texas	2.86	2.23	2.30	− .63	− .56
University of Washington	2.81	2.24	2.31	− .57	− .50
Total	2.78	2.20	2.28	− .58	− .50
Teachers Colleges					
Georgia Southern College	2.62	2.47	2.55	− .15	− .07
Kansas State College of Pittsburg	2.61	2.28	2.41	− .33	−.20
Kansas State Teachers College					
of Emporia	2.63	2.31	2.50	− .32	− .13
Central Michigan University	2.45	2.18	2.31	− .27	− .14
Eastern Michigan University	2.49	2.58	2.53	+ .08	+ .04
Western Michigan University	2.41	2.35	2.45	− .06	+ .04
State University of New York:					
College at New Paltz	2.44	2.15	2.07	− .29	− .37
College at Oswego	2.51	2.34	2.40	− .17	− .11
Sam Houston State Teachers College	2.51	2.28	2.45	− .23	− .06
Western Washington State College	2.55	2.40	2.48	− .15	− .07
Total	2.52	2.36	2.43	− .16	− .09
Other State Institutions					
Long Beach State College	2.53	2.29	2.37	− .24	− .16
San Francisco State College	2.54	2.25	2.28	− .29	− .26
Florida State University	2.59	2.35	2.49	− .24	− .10
Northern Illinois University	2.59	2.21	2.31	− .38	− .28
Southern Illinois University	2.59	2.49	2.50	− .10	− .09
Kansas State University	2.65	2.01	2.12	− .64	− .53
University of Michigan:					
Dearborn Campus	2.76	2.52	2.57	− .24	− .19
Flint Campus	2.78	2.63	2.71	− .15	− .07
Michigan State University	2.49	2.29	2.36	− .20	− .13
Wayne State University	2.44	2.37	2.38	− .07	− .06
Texas Technological College	2.78	2.23	2.38	− .55	− .40
Washington State University	2.65	2.26	2.33	− .39	− .32
Total	2.58	2.30	2.36	− .28	− .22
Private Universities					
University of Southern California	—	2.55	2.60	—	—
University of the Pacific	2.64	2.39	2.52	− .25	− .12
University of Miami	2.37	2.11	2.13	− .26	− .24
Emory University	2.72	2.16	2.37	− .56	− .35
Loyola University (Illinois)	2.64	2.34	2.38	− .30	− .26
Roosevelt University	2.48	2.00	2.06	− .48	− .42
New York University	2.74	2.22	2.24	− .52	− .50
Seattle University	2.27	2.26	2.25	− .01	− .02
Total	2.56	2.31	2.36	− .25	− .20
Technical Institutions					
Georgia Institute of Technology	2.80	1.66	1.87	−1.14	− .93
Rochester Institute of Technology	2.74	2.31	2.22	− .43	− .52
Texas A&M University	2.66	2.33	2.50	− .33	− .16
Total	2.73	2.27	2.34	− .46	− .39

* Cumulative grade point average is for the first two years after transfer (or until withdrawal if it occurred before the end of the second year).

49

differences among types, which could be only partially tested with the present data. First, there were significant differences in the quality of the students who were admitted as freshmen to the five types of institutions and with whom the junior college students competed for grades after transfer. The transfer students tended to earn their lowest grades in the four-year institutions where the quality of the native students was highest, except in the few institutions which also selected their transfer students with great care. The major state universities usually attracted the best freshmen among those attending public institutions, regardless of their formal admission standards. The teachers colleges, on the other hand, were largely unselective and attracted high school graduates with a wide range of ability. Furthermore, some teachers colleges attracted students with above average ability who later withdrew in order to transfer to university programs at the upper division level. Research is needed into the effect of raising freshman standards in four-year colleges on transfer student performance, when standards for the latter group are not changed accordingly. Some evidence to support the explanation of type differences in the quality of entering students was obtained in the present study from statements of admission policy and practice, local studies of the characteristics of entering students, and test score norms. However, a longitudinal study is needed in order to assess the long-term effect of changes in the quality of entering freshmen.

A second set of factors producing differences in transfer student performance is related to the size and complexity of the different types of colleges. Transfer students in the large universities tended to earn lower grades than those who entered small institutions, some of which resembled junior colleges. In the large public institutions in particular, less value may be placed on undergraduate instruction than on research and graduate programs, with the result that the transfer students sometimes lose interest or lack motivation to do their best work. Student advising, counseling, orientation, and other services are often neglected in large institutions, particularly at the transfer student level. Furthermore, university evaluation and grading tends to be impersonal and at times even unfair to the transfer students who lack familiarity with the "system" in which the native students have survived for two years. The teachers colleges were still quite small in 1960 and were thus able to maintain a much closer student–faculty relationship than was found in the universities. The number of different programs, departments, courses, and requirements was comparatively small and, thus, the choices to be made were also fewer in the teachers colleges. The result was that the transfer students were somewhat less bewildered by the change from what was often a small junior college in their home community. These and other factors appear to have created a kind of climate which differed in the five types of colleges and which had an important effect on the level of performance of the transfer students.

A third factor which appeared useful in interpreting differences in transfer student grades among types of colleges is the range of majors offered by the different types of institutions. Some junior colleges did not yet have adequate faculty resources or the necessary physical facilities to offer good preparation in the sciences and mathematics. Male students who transferred to the universities showed a strong preference for engineering and business adminis-tration, both of which require considerable preparation in mathe-matics. Transfers to the teachers colleges were more likely to have majors which required preparation in liberal arts fields. The differing quality of preparation of the junior college students in the various specialized majors, which was reflected in their grades after transfer, does not mean that the junior colleges *cannot* offer satis-factory preparation which would permit their students to compete in the upper division on a par with native students. The inference to be drawn from the findings is only that some junior colleges were not offering in certain fields preparation for transfer equal to that of the native students in the universities in the late 1950's.

Grade Point Differentials. There was considerable interest in the present study in the differentials obtained for the five types of four-year colleges in order to find out whether a transfer student with only a C average would have a fair probability of earning satisfac-tory grades in all institutions. The findings do not support the no-tion of equal probability (or similar differentials), either for the five types or for the forty-three participating institutions. (See Table 8.) A comparison of the mean junior college grade point average for all students who transferred to the ten teachers colleges and their cumu-lative average after transfer yielded a differential of only −0.09, which is quite near zero. On the other hand, the gross differential for the several thousand students who transferred to the major state uni-versities was −0.50, which is a serious drop in grades for students with junior college averages of only C or C+. Between the two ex-tremes, the gross differential for the other state universities as a type was found to be −0.22; for the private universities, −0.20; and for the three technical institutions, −0.39.

An examination of the differentials for individual institutions gives a somewhat less convincing picture of type differences, al-

51

though the same pattern is quite apparent. There is a considerable range in the differentials within each type, partly as a result of differences among the states. Institutional differentials tended to be larger than the gross differentials for the institutions as types. While the differentials for particular institutions will fluctuate from year to year, and among the junior colleges from which the students transfer, they appear to be useful as explanatory factors.

Differences Among the States

Graduation and Attrition. The probability that a junior college transfer student would complete a baccalaureate degree program was found to depend upon the state in which his institution is located, as well as upon individual and institutional factors. Significant differences were found among the states in both the percentages of

TABLE 9: ENROLLMENT STATUS OF THE JUNIOR COLLEGE STUDENTS THREE YEARS AFTER TRANSFER, BY STATES

STATE	NUMBER OF STUDENTS	ENROLLMENT STATUS (In percent)		
		Graduated	Still Enrolled	Dropped Out
Pennsylvania	269	72	9	19
Michigan	1,126	70	9	21
Georgia	483	70	6	24
Texas	593	65	10	25
California	2,162	63	8	29
Florida	596	63	7	30
Kansas	637	60	8	32
Washington	578	56	10	34
New York	257	58	7	35
Illinois	542	54	8	38
Total	7,243	62	9	29

students who were granted their degrees and the grade point averages they earned. The states are ordered in Table 9 on the basis of the dropouts, rather than the graduates, because of differences in the numbers of students who were still enrolled and would probably graduate in due time. The range in attrition was from 19 percent for Pennsylvania to 38 percent for Illinois. The percentage of graduates during the three-year follow-up study ranged from 54 to 72, again with Illinois and Pennsylvania at the extremes.

The factors which produced differences among the states are believed to be multiple and dynamic in the sense that they reflect the changing situation in higher education in many states. The reasons for the success of the Pennsylvania students are probably easiest to postulate. Pennsylvania State University was the only institutional participant in the study in Pennsylvania since none of the other four-year institutions admitted a significant number of full-time transfer students from junior colleges in 1960. Most of the junior college students originated on one of the Commonwealth Campuses of the university. Articulation between the Commonwealth and main campuses was close in such matters as standards for freshman admission, grading, programs, and other facets of curriculum and instruction. The students still experienced some drop in grades in moving from relatively small campuses, which were often located in their home communities, to a very large residential campus. However, they were permitted to carry their grade point balances with them from the two-year colleges. Since the balances were usually plus grade points, most students had what might be regarded as a cushion for the first term after transfer when their grades might be expected to drop. The negative side of the Pennsylvania picture is that admission to the two-year Commonwealth Campus colleges was limited to applicants who could also qualify for admission to the main university campus. High school graduates with poor records were thus denied an opportunity to demonstrate their ability to do college work in a two-year institution, although the provision of such opportunity is traditionally an important junior college function. Furthermore, the cost of education at the Commonwealth Campuses was high by usual junior college standards, even when the students could live at home while attending. Another important junior college function was thus at least partially neglected, i.e., the provision of free or low-cost education for the first two years beyond high school.

The circumstances were quite different in the two states in which the transfer students achieved the next best records. Opportunity to attend junior college in Georgia and Michigan was limited chiefly by the location of the institutions and the amount of space available in them. The University of Michigan was selective in admitting transfer students but the other universities in the state admitted most applicants with C averages. The six which participated in the study offered a wide range of liberal arts and specialized programs to meet the varied interests and needs of the transfer students. The relatively high degree of success of the Michigan junior college transfer students appears to reflect favorably on the diversity of opportunity offered by the institutions in that state.

The success of the students in Georgia appears to stem from a vastly different set of factors from those present in the Michigan and Pennsylvania situations. First, there was comparatively little overlap in the curricular opportunities offered by the four-year institutions in Georgia which participated in the study. Transfer students in engineering were forced to enter the Georgia Institute of Technology, unless they were in agricultural engineering; those in agriculture and in most business administration programs entered the University of Georgia; most men and women in teacher education transferred to Georgia Southern College; and those from Emory-at-Oxford entered the liberal arts college of Emory University in Atlanta. Native students in the various four-year colleges with whom the transfer students competed for grades differed considerably in their general academic aptitude and specialized abilities, in ways which reflected their differing vocational interests. Another factor in the Georgia picture was the influx of large numbers of transfer students from the public two-year colleges in New York State and from private junior colleges in a number of southeastern states. The record of the New York State transfer students, most of whom were enrolled in agricultural programs, was somewhat better than that of other transfer groups in terms of both on-time graduation and attrition. On the negative side of the picture, it might be pointed out, in Georgia junior college students who desire to major in engineering are very severely restricted in their opportunity to achieve both occupational and degree goals. The record of the transfer students at the Georgia Institute of Technology was rather poor and no other public institution offered programs which were at all comparable. All public two- and four-year institutions in Georgia are under a single Board of Regents for the University System, which has full responsibility for the planning and coordination of higher education in that state. However, there is at present less articulation among programs than might be expected under this type of organization of higher education at the state level.

A partial explanation of the poor Illinois record may be found in the concentration of a number of programs in advanced technical and applied fields, particularly engineering, at the University of Illinois. These programs were highly attractive to the junior college transfer students, many of them in the C to C+ grade point range where their probability of succeeding at the university was quite low. Many such students appear to have preferred risking failure there to changing their major to one offered by another university where their probability of success was somewhat higher. The two private universities in Chicago which participated in the study were also found to have rather high attrition among the transfer students. The apparent lack of success on the part of many students who transferred to these institutions was due as much to their irregular attendance patterns as to their lack of achievement. Many could not afford to enroll on a continuing full-time basis, even though they lived at home with their families. In assessing the Illinois situation, then, it might be pointed out that many high school graduates could attend a growing number of locally controlled junior colleges in 1960 and could transfer to any one of several state universities and private institutions. The main restrictions on transfer were the high tuition fees of the private institutions and the limited diversification of occupational and professional curricula in the state universities.

Few generalizations can be made for New York State from the present data because of the very small number of junior college students who transferred in 1960 and the diversity of the institutions they entered. Lack of opportunity to transfer, particularly to public institutions, appears to have been a very critical factor in the rather poor performance record of the transfer students in New York State. There was at that time no multipurpose state university like those in other states. Only a very few junior college students transferred to the specialized colleges, such as agriculture and ceramic engineering, which were supported by the state but located in private universities. The most widespread opportunity was in the teacher education programs offered by the various colleges in the State University of New York system. One possible inference from the findings is that the students who transferred to the New York State institutions which participated in the study were not necessarily the most academically able among the junior college students and that articulation between the two- and four-year colleges was rather ineffective at that time. For example, it is possible that many very able high school graduates enrolled in terminal electronics programs in the two-year colleges, since there were no state-supported programs in general engineering, while the less able male students enrolled in teacher education programs. However, an internal study of transfer in New York State tells only part of the story. Fully half the junior college transfer students entered four-year institutions in other states, where they majored in engineering, business administration, agriculture, and other specialized fields. Their record at the University of Georgia was good, but their dispersion among the other institutions was too wide to warrant attention in the present study.[1]

[1] Thomas M. Shay, *A Study of Terminal-Program Students Who Transferred in 1961 from Public Two-Year Colleges in the State of New York.* In process at the Center for the Study of Higher Education, University of California, Berkeley, 1965.

Junior college students in Washington, Kansas, and Florida made a comparatively poor showing because of the rather large number who transferred to the state universities without sufficiently good junior college records to sustain them through the first two terms after transfer. Students with only a C average in junior college had a relatively poor chance for survival at the major state universities. In 1960 these students were admitted unconditionally by these institutions, although their probability of success was much higher in other state universities which often offered the same or a similar major.

Grade Point Achievement. Differences among the ten states in the level of grades earned by the junior college transfer students were not directly related to differences in graduation and attrition rates. The degree to which good junior college grades resulted in a high rate of success after transfer appeared to depend at least in part on the effectiveness of articulation between and among the colleges in particular states. Although junior college students had fairly complete freedom in 1960 to choose among the public four-year colleges to which they might want to transfer, a considerable amount of self-selection took place in several states as a result of good counseling, articulation of programs, and communication among the colleges about student performance. In some states even students with low junior college averages (between 2.0 and 2.2) were able to achieve their degree objectives, provided they chose a four-year college which had a near-zero differential with their junior college. (See Tables 5 and 8.)

Michigan provides one such example. The mean junior college grade point average for all Michigan transfer students was among the lowest for the ten states included in the study. However, the average grades earned by transfer students in the Michigan universities were the highest among the ten states. Michigan also achieved the second-best state record based on graduation and attrition rates. Transfer students to Pennsylvania State University also earned comparatively low grades in junior college, as a group, but experienced a high degree of success after transfer, at least insofar as graduation and attrition rates are measures of success. The three states in which the students showed the highest grade point achievement both in junior college and after transfer are Texas, California, and Washington. However, they ranked only fourth, fifth, and eighth among the ten states in the percentages of their students who graduated or persisted to the end of the study. Variation among the states in the averages earned after transfer was greater than the variation in the junior college averages. However, differences among the states were statistically significant with respect to both types of averages.

Several inferences may be drawn from the state comparisons, which may require further testing in other states or at a later time. The one that is most strongly supported by the findings is that the junior colleges will be successful in performing the transfer function to the extent that they are able to disperse their students among different types of four-year colleges with different curricular offerings, grading standards, instructional methods, and other aspects of program. Still another inference is that the record of the transfer students will improve as opportunity is expanded in higher education only to the extent that:

1. Transfer students choose institutions and majors which are appropriate to their academic ability and prior achievement.

2. Diversification of opportunity to transfer is developed, i.e., occupational majors with different emphases or different levels of abstraction at several four-year institutions in each state.

3. Feedback on student performances is provided by the four-year institutions as a basis for more effective counseling about transfer, *or* selective admission standards are adopted by those institutions at which transfer students now have a low probability of success in the upper division.

Trends in Admissions

An attempt was made to document and assess the changes which had taken place in freshman and transfer admission in the four-year institutions between the time the participating students entered junior college and the fall of 1964 when the study ended. All but seven of the institutions reported some type of change at the freshman level, including increases in grade point standards and/or subject requirements, closer adherence to existing standards, improvement in the quality of students as a result of better counseling, and changes in the nature of the requirements, such as the addition of a testing program for admission. More than half the institutions reported what they regarded as significant improvements in their transfer students since 1960, resulting from either stricter admission standards or better junior college preparation, or both. Only a very few institutions became truly selective at the transfer level by requiring all applicants to present averages above C. The change, instead, was in the direction of requiring marginally qualified applicants to delay transfer or to meet some additional requirements.

There appeared to be a general expectation on the part of the four-year colleges and universities that transfer students should perform as well as native students, although this criterion was not usually invoked in establishing new admission standards.

The degree of restriction placed on the mobility of junior college transfer students in the various states will, of course, be related to the level of success to be expected in the four-year institutions. A number of the state universities are now facing severe shortages of spaces for new undergraduate students. As this occurs they will be tempted to restrict transfer opportunities by abandoning their present open-door policies for junior college students with satisfactory records. The establishment of reasonable standards and policies, and the improvement of counseling in the two- and four-year colleges with respect to transfer, are clearly a necessity if the states are to make best use of their higher education facilities.

5

Curriculum, Counseling, and Economic Problems

Findings in the areas of curriculum, counseling, and economic problems, in each of which guidelines are needed, are not as easily put in quantitative form as those in the area of student performance. And when there are statistics available, they do not necessarily point to ways of facilitating the progress of transfer students through their degree programs, reducing attrition, and increasing the learning which takes place. Needed guidelines have less to do with admission requirements and evaluation of performance than with producing the best kind of educational experience possible for the transfer students from junior college. Both questionnaire responses and information obtained from the students in interviews were used in attempting to point up strengths and weaknesses in these three areas. The problems which are suggested by the findings should be the concern of both two- and four-year colleges, in different ways and at different times.

The area of curriculum and instruction involves feedback from the junior college students about their experiences and problems in transferring to the four-year college, reasons for their failure to graduate on time, an assessment of losses of transfer credit, and policies governing the evaluation of credit. The findings about counseling include material on the importance of decision-making about college attendance and transfer, student evaluations of the help they received, problems leading to attrition after transfer, and the need for orientation in the four-year colleges. Finally, the socioeconomic thread runs through the entire story of the transfer students from junior colleges—their family backgrounds, their reasons for attending junior college, their problems after transfer, and their withdrawal from the four-year colleges.

59

Curriculum and Instruction

The transfer students as a group were exceedingly well satisfied with their junior colleges, if the reports they made both one and two years after transfer reflect their true evaluation of their experiences. They were asked by questionnaire to give several overall indications of their feelings about the junior college and then to make more specific ratings of the junior college faculty and the instruction they received. A very high percentage of the students said that they would undoubtedly make the same decision again about attending junior college as a freshman, rather than a four-year institution, if they were confronted with such a choice. In interviews they testified that the junior college experience had been good for them, personally, and they recommended it highly for other members of their family, friends, and most high school graduates. They were enthusiastic about both the quality of the junior college faculty and the range of courses offered as preparation for senior college work. They gave their most favorable ratings to their instructors' knowledge of subject matter, their ability to teach, and to their deep interest in their students. Among the many thousands who rated more than three hundred junior colleges, fewer than 10 percent said that they were quite dissatisfied with the junior college they had attended. Many of these students acknowledged that they probably would have failed if they had attended a four-year college as a freshman. Therefore, even this dissatisfied group felt that they owed a debt to the junior college. This is not to say that all instructors in all courses in every junior college taught all students equally well. However, both the generalizations and the rather specific evaluations made by the students quite some time after transfer conveyed the strong impression that they were enthusiastic advocates of the junior college.

While the students were very favorable in their evaluations of the junior college instructional program, they made a number of suggestions for improvements when encouraged to do so. The good students wanted their junior college instructors to make them work harder, particularly during the sophomore year. They expressed the idea that instruction could then be "beefed up" for students planning to transfer to the major universities. For example, they wanted to have longer and more taxing assignments, more independent study, different types of examinations and evaluations, and, in some cases, extra work which would make them better prepared for the rigors of university competition.

Evaluation of Junior College Credit. The students were questioned about their loss of credit in transferring to the four-year colleges, and very detailed analyses were made of their transcripts from the two types of institutions. While more than half lost some credit, fewer than 15 percent viewed the loss as serious. The students were much more concerned about their "loss" of junior college grade points than about small losses of course credit. Fewer than 10 percent of the students lost a substantial amount of credit, i.e., the equivalent of one semester or quarter. The major reason for loss of credit was the limitation placed by the four-year colleges on the amount which could be used to satisfy baccalaureate degree requirements—usually about half the total program. More than 20 percent received poor or failing grades in junior college, including D grades which were not accepted by some institutions as evidence of satisfactory performance. Junior college courses taken to satisfy high school deficiencies or to remedy weaknesses in basic skills accounted for the third largest category of lost credit.

On the whole, the four-year colleges which participated in the study were fairly liberal in their policies for awarding transfer credit, although most placed some restriction on the total amount of junior college credit which could be used to satisfy baccalaureate degree requirements. The limitation on amount is consistent with the conception of the junior college as a two-year, lower division institution. A few senior institutions have recently abandoned their limitation on the amount of junior college credit they will accept for transfer and, instead, specify some minimum amount which must be earned in a four-year institution. In some cases the credit may be earned in *any* four-year institution and in others there is a two-year residence requirement at the institution granting the degree.

One possible source of ambiguity is the usefulness of the credit evaluation which is made at the time of admission. At many institutions the admissions office certifies only that X amount of credit is transferable from junior college. The real evaluation of its worth in satisfying degree requirements is made much later. The question then becomes one of whether the junior college students (and others) are lulled into thinking that all their junior college courses advance them toward their degree, when in effect an unknown portion of the transferred credit can or will not be assigned in making degree checks. Despite these problems the findings from both the student questionnaires and the analysis of transcripts seem to suggest that loss of transfer credit is a serious problem for so few students that articulation efforts might well be devoted to other areas, once guidelines are established.

Efficiency in Completing Degree Programs. The native and transfer students who graduated in 1962 were compared with respect to their "efficiency" in moving through their degree programs, i.e., number of terms in which they were enrolled and the credit they earned. Excessively long periods of enrollment after transfer are costly to the student, to his parents, and to the taxpayer in the case of publicly supported institutions. Students are being diverted to the junior colleges on the assumption that the total cost of their degree programs will be no more (and probably less) than if they entered four-year colleges as freshmen. The assumption is based on costs per unit of degree credit rather than on the cost of producing a baccalaureate degree recipient. At the same time, a contrary assumption is often made that junior college students will inevitably take longer to complete their degree programs because of the many problems of curricular articulation in the several institutions. This study attempted to discover the validity of the latter assumption.

The junior college students tended to be older than the native students when they began college, to drop out from time to time (or just before transferring to the four-year college), to take time to explore different programs and courses in junior college (sometimes while making up high school deficiencies), and to enroll on a part-time basis while employed. The analysis of their relative efficiency was made, therefore, on the basis of the number of terms spent in the upper division and the total number of units earned toward the baccalaureate degree. The data show that approximately equal percentages of native and transfer students completed their degree programs in four semesters or six quarters (or less) after attaining upper division standing. The junior college group made greater use of summer sessions after entering the upper division. About 10 percent of each group also earned credit in extension, by correspondence, and/or by examination. The percentage of transfer students who completed their degree programs with about the minimum possible number of units was a little higher than the native student percentage, when total amounts of credit earned in both the two- and four-year colleges were compared. The percentage of transfer students who earned a considerable amount of credit in excess of normal degree requirements was found to be no higher than that of the native students. Eight percent of the transfer students who graduated in 1962 withdrew at some time during the upper division, compared with only 5 percent of the native students, but fewer than 2 percent of either group were dismissed for poor scholarship during their upper division years. The findings thus suggest that the graduates who originated in junior colleges were just as "efficient" as the natives in completing their baccalaureate degree programs, although some had a later and slower start than their counterparts in the four-year colleges.

Delays in Graduation and Other Problems. The records of nearly two thousand students who transferred from junior college with junior standing but who failed to graduate two years later were analyzed in depth in an attempt to discover reasons for their delay. Grade point averages, amount of credit, and satisfaction of particular degree requirements in the various majors were all examined as possible reasons. Fewer than 5 percent of the nongraduates were enrolled in five-year programs in engineering and related fields. Poor grades accounted for fewer than 20 percent of the students who were still enrolled but who did not graduate on time. Most of these students also lacked both credit and certain specific course requirements for graduation, in addition to their unsatisfactory grades. Of the nongraduates whose grade point averages were C or better, 78 percent had not earned the minimum amount of credit required for graduation in various fields. Only 15 percent with such a shortage had attempted enough units to graduate at the end of two years. Thus most of the students who did not graduate on time simply lacked enough credit to do so. This was the result of having taken less than full course loads or in a small number of cases, having failed and/or repeated courses.

An analysis was also made of the transcripts of dropouts from a small sample of colleges with rather high attrition rates in order to identify particular areas in which there was a high incidence of failure or poor grades. Transfer students who dropped out were found to have earned their poorest grades in lower division courses, often in general education courses taken after transfer in order to satisfy specific graduation requirements. Most of these courses could have been taken in junior college before transfer. Specific courses which proved to be obstacles for transfer students differed somewhat for the various colleges included in the analysis. However, foreign language and other sequence courses not completed in junior college appeared to be a common source of poor grades at a number of institutions whose records were analyzed.

Students in the various majors appeared to have about the same probability of graduation and attrition, when data from all institutions were combined, although some programs required more time than others. Most of the engineering programs were described as four-year curricula in the catalogs of the various institutions but the students often required more than two years after transfer to complete them. However, the transfers did not differ from the native students in the upper division in this regard. Some students in teacher education programs also needed additional time to complete their programs of degrees and credentials because of student teaching requirements which took them away from the campus during most of one term.

Articulation of programs in the two- and four-year colleges is becoming increasingly complex as a result of a number of factors, among them the evolution of the teachers colleges into multipurpose institutions, increased selectivity by the universities at the freshman and transfer levels, and new residence hall programs, all of which have the effect of spreading the junior college transfer students out among the several four-year colleges in each state. Each four-year college usually has its own general education requirements, different sequences of courses, and other variations in curriculum. Formerly, many junior colleges aligned their programs with those of the major state university to which most of their students transferred. However, new patterns of transfer are emerging which will probably lead to a reduction of the flow of students into the major state universities and a great increase in the number transferring to other types of institutions.

A second area of concern is the need for better articulation of instructional methods in high school and junior college and in junior college and four-year institutions. While the junior colleges appear to have minimized the shock of moving from high school to college, they were less effective in preparing their students for the shock of transferring to large universities where teaching methods differed from those used in both high school and junior college.

Counseling and Advising

The transfer students gave much less favorable ratings to the counseling and academic advising they received in junior college than they did to various aspects of the instructional program. However their opinions of junior college counseling and advising were more favorable than their feelings toward comparable services in the four-year institutions to which they transferred. A large percentage of the students reported that they had not received personal counseling at either type of institution. Furthermore, some who had adjustment problems after transfer were not aware of counseling services available to them. Many equated "counseling" with program planning, which it sometimes was in the junior college. It appears that students who knew what they wanted to do, in terms of their major and the institution to which they planned to transfer, were programmed accordingly by counselors or advisers in the junior college without reference to their academic ability or prior achievement. Apparently too little attention was given to evaluation during counseling sessions held after the students had had some experience in transfer programs in junior college to see whether a change in major and/or transfer institution might be indicated. In general, the feeling of the students was that the counseling and/or advising they received was too infrequent and the sessions too short, rather than that the services were poor. At the universities, in particular, transfer students had unsatisfactory experiences with their faculty advisers, who were generally unfamiliar with the junior colleges, often disinterested in their advisees, and seldom available for consultation when the students felt the need for it.

The need for counseling about college at all levels of education was pointed up by the finding that an early decision to attend college was positively related to low attrition after transfer and to a high probability of on-time graduation. The groups which were the exceptions to this generalization were the men who made up their minds to attend college while in military service (and who did very well afterward in college), and those who made early decisions to attend particular universities where they proved unable to handle the work. In other words, an early decision was good only if it was an appropriate one in terms of the student's developing capacity to do work at a particular level. Among high school graduates who were ill equipped for lower division work at a university, some who attended junior college made up their deficiencies and went on to transfer with good records, while others achieved at only a minimally acceptable level in junior college and were dismissed for poor scholarship shortly after transfer. Students who decided to transfer to a particular four-year institution by the end of their freshman year in junior college experienced much greater success than students who delayed their decision until they completed their junior college programs. The timing of career decisions, however, was not clearly related to success, perhaps because the students had not yet decided upon a particular type of work when they answered the questions about careers.

Approximately equal percentages of students said they had made their initial decision to attend college in elementary school, early in high school, and after graduating from high school. Women tended to make earlier decisions than men. The men who decided to attend college after graduating from high school but had no intervening experience, e.g., military service or employment, had high attrition after transfer, often with rather poor grades. They usually were not prepared for college when they graduated from high school, either in the courses they had taken or the quality of work they had achieved. The findings seem to point up the need for high school and college counselors to work together in helping students make long-range college plans, with built-in evaluations from time to time to test the feasibility of the plans.

Nearly one-fourth of the transfer students said that uncertainty about their plans for a major or a career field was a factor of considerable importance in their decision to attend junior college, rather than a four-year institution, after high school. Nearly one-third said that a feeling of not being prepared for senior college work was of at least some importance in their decision. The importance of these reasons for attending junior college was confirmed in interviews with the students a year later. Many had not wanted to risk their academic futures in four-year colleges until they were somewhat more certain about their interests and motivations for undertaking a baccalaureate degree program. More than one-fourth of the students who had chosen majors before they entered junior college changed them before transferring to four-year institutions. The largest single shift was out of engineering, often into business administration. A full 30 percent of the changes in major made by the men in junior college involved engineering. As they moved through their junior college programs, some of the men weighed their early decision to major in engineering against their poor lower division grades in courses in mathematics and science and decided to transfer to colleges which did not offer engineering. One-fourth of the students said that they were not committed to particular majors when they finished their junior college work. However, the stability of their majors in the four-year institutions, once chosen, was relatively high. Only 16 percent of the students changed majors after transfer. Most of these students made only one change. Women were somewhat more prone to make several changes, many of them as a result of their lack of awareness of the multiple opportunities available to them in the major state universities. Nearly two-thirds of the women planned to enter the teaching field after graduation, compared with one-fourth of the men.

Attrition after Transfer in Relation to Counseling. A very large number of the students who said that they attended junior college because of uncertainty about their interests or motivation for baccalaureate degree work dropped out after transfer. Their comments in the spring after transfer on their adjustment to the four-year college showed the probability of their dropping out some time later. In their questionnaires they expressed doubt that they had made a wise choice of college and apparently felt free to say that they expected to drop out. The questionnaires they completed after withdrawing from college contained lengthy passages concerning their renewed doubts about their ability, the value of the education they were receiving, their interest in their major or chosen occupation, or their values. Many said that they were dropping out "in order to think things over," after which they might return to college to complete their degree programs. Some were frank to say that other values had become more important to them than a baccalaureate degree—marriage and family for the women, remunerative employment opportunities for the men.

The dropouts were asked whether they had attempted to seek help before (or at the time of) their decision to withdraw. They were asked for details concerning the person from whom they sought help and the value of the help they received. The replies were disheartening. Apparently counseling was often limited to students who were in need of therapy, many of whom were advised to drop out of college to get it. Students with everyday problems of doubts about their motivation and interest seldom seemed to find help at the four-year colleges and universities. Many of them were mature students who felt the need to weigh their decisions about continuing in college very carefully. Whether they actually re-enrolled in college or transferred to other institutions at a later time was not fully known at the end of the three-year follow-up study.

Other Aspects of Student Personnel Services. Orientation programs for transfer students were largely unsuccessful. In most instances the students were grouped with the freshmen, sometimes unintentionally and at other times on the assumption that the needs of both groups could be served in a common program. The program was often offered before the opening of the fall semester when a large number of the transfer students were still employed in their home communities, earning money for their expenses for the fall semester. Many of them were married when they transferred and expressed interest in an orientation program which would include their wives because of their need to understand what the life of an upper division university student is like. There was general agreement among the transfer students who participated in orientation programs that the present ones are unsatisfactory. Some students were not aware that programs were offered; others felt no need to participate. While a significant number of students thought that orientation was needed for junior college transfers, they had not given much thought to the kind of program they wanted. Apparently this is an area which needs study on individual campuses, in cooperation with junior colleges from which the transfer students come. It is possible that orientation during the semester before transfer would be more helpful than the usual fall program, particularly if the student's major department would be willing to assist in orientation during the first semester after transfer.

In filling out questionnaires the students tended to deny that social problems were a source of poor adjustment after transfer. However, in interviews many of the students cited this type of problem as one of the disadvantages of attending a junior college. Two factors tend to discourage transfer students from participating in social and extracurricular activities. First, the transfer students remarked that recruitment into many special interest groups appeared to be directed toward new freshmen. The second factor tending to discourage the transfer students, particularly in the universities, was their felt need to devote all their time to their studies during their first semester after transfer in order to earn passing grades. After that semester, they tended to feel that it was too late to start participating in activities programs. Many junior college student leaders became almost totally inactive after transfer when they failed to find assignments open to them for which they did not have to compete with freshmen. On the whole, the transfer students—except those in church groups—tended to have much less identity with the four-year colleges than did their native student classmates in the upper division.

Summary on the Need for Better Counseling. The counseling function might be regarded as equal in importance to instruction in the junior college, at least to the very large numbers of students who enter with no clear notion of what they hope to achieve, nor of their ability to achieve the various objectives open to them. The choices high school graduates must make are increasing in both number and complexity as educational opportunity expands. Students must choose among several colleges, most of which offer programs in their fields of interest; between a two- and four-year college, both of which may be located within commuting distance of home; between borrowing under the NDEA loan program in order to go away to college and attending a local junior college; between dropping out after high school in order to earn money to attend college full time and enrolling part time or at night while employed; and when to transfer to a four-year college, if they start their program in a junior college. The idea is beginning to gain acceptance that there may be a number of tenable routes to the baccalaureate degree, rather than only one traditional track "from high school to four-year college as a full-time student, until withdrawal or graduation four years later." High school and college counselors in all types of institutions will need more than ever to work together to assist students and their parents in evaluating the various choices and in adopting the plan best suited to their particular capabilities, financial resources, and interests.

The Economic Plight of the Junior College Students

One of the threads running through the entire study is the economic plight of the junior college students who transfer to four-year institutions. The thread begins with the characteristics of the students and their families, continues through their decisions about college attendance and career choice, appears again in the problems they encountered after transfer, and ends, perhaps, with the story of their attrition after transfer. Their handicap is affected variously by programs, policies, and practices in the four-year colleges which both alleviate and aggravate the financial problems the students face in undertaking transfer programs leading to their baccalaureate degrees.

In many ways the junior college transfer students resembled what is regarded as the typical undergraduate student in public four-year colleges and universities, except in their social class membership. The parents of the junior college students were less well educated than those of the natives, and the employment and income of their fathers reflected this difference. The transfer students, particularly the women, tended to come from larger families than the native students. They were more likely to be self-supporting during college. Nearly 20 percent of the male transfer students reported that they paid nearly all their college costs out of their own earnings, compared with only 8 percent of the native students. About 40 percent of the men in the transfer group—as against one-third of the men in the native group—said that their parents contributed nothing toward paying for their college education. About three-fourths of the transfer men and slightly fewer than half the women reported that they used some portion of their own earnings from part-time and summer work to pay for the cost of their education. Incidence of time-consuming employment after transfer was somewhat less than expected. Apparently the students feared that employment would seriously interfere with their university studies if they were to continue it at the same level as in junior college. About twice as many students worked while attending junior college as in the first year after transfer; the number of hours worked per week was also much larger in junior college.

The reasons which the largest numbers of students gave for choosing the junior college were low cost, location of the college in their home communities, and opportunity for employment while attending college. Far fewer students gave what might be called positive reasons for choosing junior college, e.g., the program offered or the informal atmosphere.

Three types of transfer students with financial problems who later encountered academic difficulty emerged from the analysis of characteristics and performance data. The first type was the employed junior college student who failed to study in either high school or junior college. If he chose his courses wisely and conformed to his instructors' expectations, he usually received C grades and was permitted to transfer to a four-year college. Even if his employment ceased after transfer, he found himself in academic trouble, for he had failed to learn how to study in junior college and did not have a good record of achievement behind his C grades. The second type was the student who had dropped out between junior college and the four-year institution, usually in order to work full time to earn money to transfer. He made a wise decision not to work after transfer, but in the period between colleges he had lost some of his study skills. Therefore, in spite of his good junior college record and dedication to study after transfer, he encountered academic difficulty because he did not have refresher work before entering a four-year institution. Courses in science and mathematics appear to be critical for such students, particularly if they enroll in upper division courses in these same fields. The third type transferred to the university with only enough money saved to carry him through the first semester. If he was typical, his grades dropped as much as a half grade point during the first semester. Therefore, it was difficult for him to secure financial aid or part-time employment for the second semester because of his academic record after transfer.

Problems after Transfer. The problem which the largest percentage of students rated as serious during the spring semester after transfer was the increased cost of their education in the four-year institution, in comparison with junior college costs and in relation to their expectations. Many students reported in interviews that they had made very unrealistic estimates of the cost of attending college away from home, particularly if they had to live in off-campus housing. Many were unable to secure part-time employment after transfer to meet their increased expenses, partly because of the type of community in which the college was located and partly because of policies which tended to discriminate against new students at both the freshman and transfer levels. The students had little money when they transferred and were unaccustomed to having a budget for their own personal needs away from home. Housing was a problem on many university campuses, particularly for those with limited funds. Jobs which were available paid only enough for spending money and did not enable the students to save for later semesters.

Among the students who dropped out voluntarily after transfer, financial problems ranked first among the various factors associated with withdrawal. Forty percent of the students checked "lack of money" as one reason for withdrawing. The supplementary information given by the students on their questionnaires tended to confirm the reality of their financial problems, although one might ask why such problems could not have been anticipated before transfer. Among the explanations were those of married men with sometimes unexpected family illness, including loss of income due to the pregnancy of the wives who were working. Other students finally recognized the impossibility of working at jobs on a full-time basis and making satisfactory grades at the same time; they had no real choice since they could not attend college without the money they were earning. Others frankly admitted that they had been confronted with promising business or employment opportunities which they valued somewhat more highly than their baccalaureate degrees.

Another category of financial dropouts were the disappointed loan seekers who transferred with the expectation of having a better chance for securing financial aid from the college after the first semester. Many had been led to believe that their chances would be good if they could earn satisfactory grades, not realizing that much of the college's loan fund was committed for the entire academic year. Others withdrew after failing to meet the conditions of athletic or other special scholarships awarded them at the time they transferred. The grade point differential suffered by most transfer students was the major deterrent to financial solvency—it was difficult for them to qualify for financial aid after such a drop and they were frightened by the drop to the point that they felt compelled to give up their part-time jobs.

Opportunity vs. Frustration. One of the major contributions of the junior college has been the offering of opportunity in higher education to capable high school graduates who could not otherwise attend college because of their limited economic resources.

There is some reason to believe that many students are thus encouraged to attend college and to develop what are probably unrealistic expectations and aspirations about transfer. It is somewhat unlikely that they will have any greater financial capability at the time they transfer than they had when they graduated from high school. Yet they are attempting to undertake upper division programs under various financial arrangements which appear to have only short-term value. It seems to be widely believed that no one drops out of college for financial reasons or, perhaps, that there is no need for any student to do so. The present study tells little about the financial needs of the would-be transfer student who never enters a four-year college. However, the various types of evidence about the financial situations of those who did in fact transfer leave no doubt that the financial handicap which a large proportion of students suffer is a real one.

6

Articulation and Coordination

THE deep concern with institutional cooperation felt by the Joint Committee on Junior and Senior Colleges and by the three associations which the members represent is reflected in the titles of the research reports of the two studies, both of which include the phrase "articulation and coordination." One might then ask why so little space has been devoted to this topic in either report, in comparison with the attention given to student performance and institutional characteristics. The answer lies in the low level of activity found in the forty-three colleges and ten states in 1960 when the junior college students transferred to the four-year institutions, and in 1964 when the study was completed. A considerable increase in interest occurred during these four years, both in informal, voluntary articulation between and among colleges and in the formal, often legally mandated coordination of all public colleges and universities in particular states. As 1964 ended, the area of formal coordination was more fluid and dynamic than at any time during the study, with a number of proposals for coordination being readied for introduction during the 1965 sessions of various state legislatures.

The lack of extensive statewide activity in articulation has been a reflection of two sets of circumstances. First, the four-year colleges have had a long history of articulation activities and programs involving the high schools from which they draw their freshmen. Attention has been focused on high school relations for so long that the colleges find it difficult to readjust their thinking and programs to the needs of the transfer students. A number of the four-year colleges which participated in the study had made no prior count of their junior college transfer students and had little idea of the volume, major sources, or success of those admitted. Until recently the number of new freshman applicants from high school was so much greater than the number of transfer students that the comparative lack of attention to college-level articulation on the part of some institutions was perhaps justified. However, the relative proportions of new freshmen and transfer students are rapidly changing as a result of the establishment of new junior colleges, the strengthening of existing ones, tightening of admission standards and increased costs in the four-year institutions, and various other factors. The second circumstance which has tended to discourage articulation among all colleges at the state level has been the concentration of junior college transfers in the major state universities. As a result, most of these institutions have developed techniques and programs for working with the junior colleges which are their major suppliers of transfer students, but have not usually involved other types of four-year colleges except as they, too, send transfer students. The latter colleges have often had too few transfer students in the past to justify the use of staff time for articulation activities with the junior colleges.

Coordination was in its infancy during the early years of the study. The Coordinating Council for Higher Education was just getting under way in California after adoption of the Master Plan for Higher Education by the legislature in 1960. The Board of Higher Education in Illinois was established in 1961 as the coordinating agency for the state universities and was assigned responsibility for developing a state master plan to be presented to the legislature in 1965. In Florida new state universities and junior colleges were being established and other changes were taking place in that system of higher education which had a profound effect on the work and responsibilities of the Board of Control for the public universities and the State Board of Education for the junior colleges. There has, of course, been a long history of coordination of a somewhat different nature in Georgia, Pennsylvania, and New York which contrasts quite sharply with the new type of coordination which is developing in California and Illinois, and perhaps in Michigan and Texas. In these four latter states, coordination will involve several different systems of state institutions and their governing boards, e.g., in California the public junior colleges, the state colleges, and the university with its several campuses. Private universities are also represented on California's Coordinating Council, as well as the state at large. In Georgia, on the other hand, the public two- and four-year colleges are all coordinated by a single Board of Regents for the University System which has fairly direct control over the individual institutions which comprise the system. Similarly, in Pennsylvania in the early 1960's coordination of two- and four-year colleges was facilitated by having the junior colleges operated as branch campuses of the state university, offering both technical and transfer programs. Coordination machinery in New York was unique because of the nature of the State University of New York and its relationship with the University of the State of New York, and because of the state's high degree of dependence upon the private segment of higher education in its planning and coordination.

The legally constituted coordination of systems of higher education in the several states is still too new to merit much consideration at this time, at least in the context of the performance of transfer students from two-year colleges. Articulation, on the other hand, has developed to the point where various models and practices which may be relevant to student performance can be described in some detail. Articulation and coordination may in fact be contrasted in terms of their differing concerns—articulation centered on the students and their courses of study and coordination on institutional budgets and building programs. Coordinating agencies tend to represent the interests of the state and its citizenry; articulation programs consider the interests of the individual student and his instructors. The major goal of statewide coordination, stated variously as the orderly development of opportunity in higher education while making good use of the state's resources, obviously overlaps with the goals of articulation. However, only time will tell what will be the distinct roles, functions, and areas of concern of articulation and coordination, and whether both types of machinery are necessary and desirable.

The Elements of Articulation

Problem Areas. Articulation, whether between pairs of programs or colleges, among groups of institutions, or at the state level, involves problems, people, and procedures. Four major problem areas are involved in articulation between the two- and four-year colleges and, to a lesser extent, the high schools insofar as college-bound students need to do long-range planning.[1] These problems deal with (1) the student, (2) curriculum and instruction, (3) student personnel services, and (4) facilities and resources. A few examples of stu-

---

[1] Material has been adapted from a paper presented at the 19th National Conference on Higher Education of the Association for Higher Education, Chicago, April 1964. A brief version of the paper has been published in *Current Issues in Higher Education, 1964,* under the title, "How Can Two- and Four-Year Colleges Provide Articulation in the Face of Rapid Changes?" (Washington: Association for Higher Education, 1964), pp. 216–19.

dent-centered problems are his choice of program, degree goals, and attendance pattern in pursuit of these goals; his academic and economic resources; and the characteristics and requirements of the colleges to which he might be admitted. Problems in the area of curriculum and instruction include the acceptance of transfer credit, the coordination of methods and materials in teaching, grading standards, course and classroom experimentation, and the preparation of teachers. In the student personnel services area, examples of problems are the coordination of financial aid programs, orientation programs for transfer students, exchanges of information about college characteristics and programs to improve counseling, and exchanges of information about students to facilitate adjustment to the transfer institutions. Finally, problems in facilities and resources, which begin to overlap with the concerns of formal coordination, are the establishment of enrollment quotas and priorities in the four-year colleges, the diversion of students to two-year colleges, differentiation in specialized programs in the two types of institutions, and the coordination of academic calendars, particularly as year-round operations are undertaken.

A few of the substantive questions which might be suitable topics for articulation conferences (or for guidelines for transfers) are these:

1. What type of admission standards for transfer students seems most appropriate in achieving articulation goals—nonselective admission of all transfer applicants with a C average in junior college? selective admission according to specified, objective standards? or selective admission at the discretion of the four-year colleges, according to quite general criteria? What weight should be given to junior college recommendations? to the high school record? to test scores?

2. How much faculty and/or institutional autonomy in matters of curriculum and instruction is possible in a highly coordinated system of two- and four-year colleges? In what areas should it be encouraged? What steps can be taken to insure that all institutions are allowed this autonomy, and particularly to avoid having the universities usurp the privilege of autonomy in instructional matters?

3. What kind of articulation is desirable in the administration of scholarships, loans, and other financial aid programs? Should potential scholarship recipients be encouraged to attend junior college for one or two years in their home communities, with a promise of aid at the time of transfer?

4. What priority should be given to junior college transfer applicants when facilities at the four-year colleges are limited and enrollments restricted? What kind of planning can be done by all segments of higher education to make sure that high school graduates attend the type of college which is best suited to their needs and abilities, and to preserve the right of students to transfer into the upper division to continue their degree programs with a minimum loss of time and credit?

Who Will Do It? Articulation involves people as well as problems and procedures. The selection of problems for articulation determines only in part the types of college personnel who should be involved in various articulation activities. The uncertainty about who should do the articulating may in some instances have delayed the development of more comprehensive statewide machinery. Examples could be cited where registrars and admission officers have assumed major responsibility for articulation among colleges. Special staff members for college relations are now being added to admissions staffs, and it seems quite likely that an even greater amount of articulation activity will be centered in that office. Elsewhere articulation has become the concern of college student personnel groups, particularly counselors. In some fields, faculty members work on articulation problems in their professional associations, e.g., in engineering and business administration. In Florida and California, where quite extensive statewide articulation programs have been developed, college administrators at a fairly high policy-making level are involved in articulation, particularly in the planning and coordination phases of state programs. Students have seldom (if ever) been directly involved in articulation at the state level although their possible contribution is worth considering.

The question then becomes one of selecting appropriate people to be involved in different types of activities—selecting problems for articulation efforts, study committees, and research; proposing and ratifying agreements; and carrying out agreements. The "who" question involves the segments of education to be represented, as well as the types of personnel. Some of the possible (and necessary) groups are the various types of public two- and four-year colleges, private institutions, high schools, state departments of education, professional associations of administrators and faculty members, regional accrediting associations, and coordinating agencies. As the number of different types of participants, as well as the gross number of colleges and universities, increases, the question of representation from each segment becomes important. When numbers require that representation be substituted for full participation by all colleges in various articulation activities, problems of rotation of responsibility among colleges and of continuity and communication arise. The major dimensions of the "who" question appear to be these: top level administrators vs. support staff (e.g., in admissions and records) vs. faculty; public institutions vs. private institutions vs. agencies and associations in higher education.

How to Make It Work. Matters of procedure or mechanics are perhaps the most complicated of all to deal with. A very fundamental question concerns the relative advantages of voluntary and compulsory articulation machinery and, if the former, how firm agreements can be reached to which all parties will be committed. In either case the mechanics are yet to be worked out for the effective communication of both information and agreements to all institutions and to all appropriate staff members within particular institutions. Under existing arrangements, agreements are sometimes made by college administrators who have no responsibility for and little information about the area concerned, e.g., in admissions and evaluation of credit. At other times curriculum agreements are reached without appropriate participation by and/or communication with faculty members and academic advisers who are expected to abide by them. Care needs to be taken in establishing statewide machinery that problems which are the concern of pairs of colleges (or of a particular four-year college and the junior colleges, or of colleges in particular service areas) do not occupy the time of the entire group of participants. Neither should statewide programs replace entirely the efforts of particular institutions in working with and offering services to the two-year colleges from which the largest numbers of their transfer students come.

Examples of Programs and Practices

The California Approach. California and Florida appear at present to have the most complete models for articulation of any of the ten states in the study. Reasons for this more advanced stage of development in California include the great dependence placed on the California junior colleges for lower division instruction, the large number of public four-year colleges to which the students transfer, the volume of transfer students in the various colleges, and the long history of voluntary cooperation among the public institutions. The California model is not presented as unique or ideal, but as one rather complex set of machinery for voluntary articulation. It differs from the Florida model in that it is not an organ of a legally constituted coordinating agency. The Articulation Conference, which is the heart of the California model, was established in 1944, many years before the creation of the Coordinating Council. The Florida Professional Committee for Relating Public Secondary and Higher Education is an organ of the State Board of Education and was established in 1957 when the volume of junior college transfer students was still quite small.

The California Articulation Conference is a quadripartite group of representatives appointed by the Junior College Association, the Association of Secondary School Administrators, the state colleges, and the university. The objective of the conference is "to coordinate publicly supported education so that California students will be afforded the quantity, quality, and variety of education commensurate with their abilities so that when desirable they can move readily from one segment to another. To achieve this end, the members or committees meet to exchange points of view, to identify problems, and to develop and recommend to appropriate authorities . . . methods for improving articulation."[2] Staff from the State Department of Education also participate in the various activities, and a representative of the relatively new Coordinating Council for Higher Education has recently been added to the membership. The conference is essentially a voluntary organization of representatives appointed by the various segments of public education, including the secondary schools, with no authority to make binding agreements or commitments. A fifteen-member administrative committee arranges programs for annual meetings, acts as a clearinghouse for matters referred by members and outside agencies, establishes and receives reports of committees of the conference, performs follow-up functions on agreements involving several segments, and serves other coordinating functions for the entire conference.

Much of the work of the conference is done by committees whose membership extends far beyond the official representation from each segment. Standing committees have been working in the fields of agriculture, business administration, engineering, foreign language, letters and science, and nursing. In addition to their regular meetings, a number of these subject-matter committees have sponsored conferences which have been attended by faculty members from a large number of two- and four-year colleges. Special committees have also been appointed from time to time to work on problems involving foreign students, the training of college teachers, the revi-

[2] Mimeographed statement adopted by the Administrative Committee of the Articulation Conference, April 23, 1963.

79

sion of transfer admission requirements, and college advisement programs, among others.

The effectiveness of the conference in reaching important agreements has been limited in the following ways:

1. It is nearly impossible to secure the views of the nearly one hundred public two- and four-year colleges in California which are parties to the conference. The three public segments of higher education are each limited to nine representatives in the conference proper, although the number of state colleges whose interests must be represented is now seventeen and the number of junior colleges more than seventy.

2. Members of the conference, including the Administrative Committee, lack authority to make agreements although they are official representatives of the various segments of public education. No penalties have been devised for the abrogation of agreements.

3. Communication is not always effective, either with the institutions without representation in the conference at the time the agreements are made or with particular staff members in the institutions who should implement the agreements, e.g., faculty members, admissions officers, and counselors.

The California Articulation Conference has been subject to considerable self-study and critical evaluation during the past two years, with some resulting changes in format and procedures. Change continues to take place, but it appears quite certain that the conference will retain its major function as a forum and clearinghouse for a wide range of problems involving the secondary schools and colleges. It is still too early to know what kind of relationship will develop between the conference and the Coordinating Council. It seems inevitable that some overlap will occur in their concerns with problems of undergraduate admission and transfer, curriculum and instruction, and student personnel services programs.

Both the University of California and the state colleges perform certain additional articulation functions quite independently in working with the high schools and junior colleges in their service areas. The university program is probably the more complete of the two because of the amount of staff time devoted to it on each campus and in the statewide Office of the University Dean of Educational Relations. The university program includes annual conferences to which junior college counselors and others are invited to discuss transfer problems of mutual interest, visitation to and by the junior colleges, publication of a periodic newsletter and a series of informational brochures of interest to counselors and students, annual studies of transfer student performance at the university which include grade point data for each junior college, and special conferences in particular disciplines for faculty members in all types of colleges. The state colleges are usually included in invitations extended to the junior colleges and in the annual performance studies because of the large numbers of their students who transfer to the university for upper division programs in specialized fields not offered elsewhere. The type of articulation program in which the University of California engages is quite similar to those offered by other major state universities, notably the University of Michigan, University of Illinois, and University of Washington, all of which are located in states with far less extensive statewide activity than California.

Other State Programs. Florida is probably the only other participating state with an extensive set of machinery at the state level for articulation between high school and college and among colleges. The program encompasses a wide spectrum of professional activities and interests. The Committee for Relating Public Secondary and Higher Education includes representatives from the secondary schools, the junior colleges, the five state universities, the Board of Control for the state universities, the Institute for Continuing University Study, the State Department of Education, and the office of the State Superintendent of Instruction. One of the major accomplishments of the committee has been the securing of an agreement governing the acceptance of transfer credit for general education programs offered by the several junior colleges and required by the universities. The policy serves both to encourage local curriculum development and to insure that the junior college credit earned by the transfer students will be recognized by the state universities in satisfaction of their particular general education requirements. The policy provides that students who have been certified by their junior college as having completed the locally prescribed general education program will not be required to enroll in additional lower division general education courses after transfer. Two conditions must be met by the junior colleges in order to qualify: they must publish their general education programs in their catalogs and the programs must include not less than thirty-six semester hours in such areas as communications, mathematics, social sciences, humanities, and natural sciences. The committee also has successfully secured the adoption of guidelines for transfer by members of the Florida Association of Colleges and Universities, including the private institutions.

Machinery for articulation and coordination in Georgia is considerably less complex than in other states because all public institutions are under a single governing board. Articulation in Georgia is accomplished through a series of administrative and academic committees of the University System Advisory Council. The various subject-matter areas are represented on the academic committees, with faculty members from each institution constituting the membership. Administrative committees have functioned in the areas of testing, records, guidance, and standards of scholarship; academic personnel; educational policy at the junior college level; and general extension. One of the most promising examples of the kind of coordination achieved in the Georgia system is the statewide program of precollege testing and guidance which was started in 1957. A guidance committee was established at each two- and four-year college in the system, with representation on a statewide committee. The program has been administered through the Regents' Office of Testing and Guidance, which prepares an annual bulletin for counselors and admissions officers with a wealth of information about the characteristics of students who enter each college. Still another very informative publication of the Regents' Office is a monograph, *Educational Opportunities and Financial Aid in the University System of Georgia,* with details on programs of study, scholarships, loans, and employment opportunities afforded by each college. A third type of publication is the *Newsletter* of the Office of Testing and Guidance, which includes extensive reviews of relevant research and publications of interest to college counselors and admissions officers, as well as news and announcements from member colleges. Communication is one of the major problems in articulation among colleges, and Georgia appears to have made a considerable effort to maintain and improve communication between the Regents' Office and the colleges in the University System.

Examples of Specific Practice in Articulation. A number of promising articulation practices developed by particular four-year institutions appear worthy of consideration by other institutions which are either beginning or trying to improve their articulation programs. The first area involves various attempts to improve communication among the colleges by means of informational brochures, course equivalency lists, guidance materials, and reports of studies of junior college transfer students. Both the University of Washington and Washington State University prepare detailed listings of parallel courses and programs for each junior college in the state and for each area of instruction as a supplement to the regular university bulletins. The objective of the publications is to aid junior college teachers, guidance workers, and others in counseling students who plan to transfer to either university, but not to standardize or to freeze the curriculum in either the two- or the four-year institutions. The published programs are viewed as guides rather than inflexible courses of study. A similar type of publication is prepared by the Los Angeles city school system for its several junior colleges in relation to the four-year institutions in southern California to which the students may transfer. Not all administrators voice wholehearted approval of this type of communication; some fear that it may bring about an undesirable degree of rigidity in both types of colleges. However, many junior college personnel appear to favor the development of such a listing of parallel courses and programs, at least until such time as appropriate guidelines for the transfer of credit and the satisfaction of various types of requirements can be established.

Another type of publication which has begun to make a more frequent appearance is the special admissions brochure for the recruitment and/or guidance of junior college transfer students. The University of Michigan, University of Texas, and University of Miami have all prepared special materials which are designed to inform both students and counselors in the junior colleges about what the universities are like and what special requirements and policies the students must be familiar with in making plans for transfer. Periodic newsletters prepared by a number of universities also serve a communications function; however, they are designed less with the transfer student in mind than the college administrator and his staff, who are not always in direct contact with the students and their counselors for whom the material should have the most value. Proceedings from subject-matter conferences also serve an important communications function for faculty and staff who do not participate in such conferences. The information exchanged and the agreements reached in such sessions should be communicated to all colleges whose students are likely to transfer to one or another of the institutions in the state.

A rather unusual articulation practice is the annual spring conference held by the student government associations of the Commonwealth and main campuses of the Pennsylvania State University, under the auspices of the Office of Student Affairs. Student leaders from the various two-year campuses meet with leaders from the main campus to discuss problems of mutual concern, plan special programs and conferences, confer with university staff, and exchange ideas. The conference serves the purpose of integrating and organizing the leadership of the branch campuses in such a way that students are able to start assuming leadership roles soon after transfer to the main campus, without the frustrating period of adjustment which usually accompanies a move from a two-year to a university campus.

The University of Miami provides a remarkable example of a private institution which has responded to the transfer needs of both local public junior colleges and nationally known private two-year colleges. The university first expanded its articulation program in response to the establishment of Miami-Dade Junior College and Florida Atlantic University, both of which are located nearby. Recently a program of new scholarships for transfer students from junior colleges was established. Though a private institution, Miami is attempting to serve the fast-growing public junior college movement in Florida by working with the new junior college in its area and with others in the state interested in its program.

Finally, the "all college day open house" of Texas A&M University should be mentioned as an exciting articulation practice. High school days have been conducted by a very large number of colleges for many years. However, the transfer students tend to have been neglected in such programs, although many who were interviewed regarded the personal trips they made to the campus before transfer as the best preparation for the transition from the two- to the four-year colleges. Junior college students and their counselors have been invited to the Texas A&M campus in the spring each year to learn about the college and its various programs and to talk with advisers. They are offered housing in the college dormitories and are treated as guests of the college for the day. To keep the spring conference focused on the prospective transfer students, administrators are invited to a completely separate conference in the fall of each year.

Feedback from Students

At the conclusion of the interviews with the transfer students, they were asked whether anyone from their junior colleges had ever asked them about their transfer problems and experiences, as had been done in the interviews in connection with the study. If not, they were asked whether they felt that such interviews would have served a useful purpose. There was a high degree of unanimity in their responses—very few of the students had ever been approached by their junior colleges for interviews and most felt that they could have made specific suggestions which would make it easier for other students to transfer to their four-year colleges. The students made it clear that their junior colleges did not lack interest in their transfer experiences but merely failed to make any systematic attempt to appraise the problems their students encountered, at least some of which could have been remedied by the junior colleges. They spoke of chance encounters with their former instructors and others from the junior colleges in which such problems were discussed—certain material which should have been covered in transfer courses, for example—but they voiced the strong opinion that they could have been more helpful if someone had taken time to talk with them during their first year after transfer.

The other aspect of articulation which the students stressed in interviews was the need for much better—and more—information about the colleges to which they were transferring. Apparently they found pretransfer visits very helpful in becoming acquainted with the campus of the four-year colleges, particularly when they could talk with advisers in their field of interest. Much necessary information could probably be obtained more efficiently in written form. The colleges should recognize that the needs of transfer students are different from those of entering freshmen who may not yet know what their interests are. The mistakes made by some transfer students as a result of wrong or poor information often resulted in considerable hardship, such as not knowing that the four-year college to which they transferred did not offer a major in the students' field of interest, failure to complete lower division requirements which could and should have been met before transfer, lack of realistic information about costs of attending, and failure to realize when they were in academic difficulty. Communication again emerged as a major problem in the students' view of articulation, i.e., communication both among colleges and between the students and the colleges they were planning to attend.

Better articulation at all levels is needed to protect the mobility of good students who will transfer for one or several reasons, to preserve institutional freedom to experiment and innovate, and to encourage all students to strive for the highest level of education they feel capable of achieving. Articulation should seek to remove barriers and obstacles to mobility, both real and imagined. Unless the two- and four-year colleges really believe that it is necessary to work together to remove these obstacles, articulation can scarcely be made to work under any type of arrangement, voluntary or otherwise.

7

Conclusions and Implications[1]

IN attempting to make as thorough as possible the assessment of transfer student performance, conclusions were drawn which deal with the nature of the students who begin their baccalaureate degree programs in two-year colleges; with conditions, policies, services, programs, and other aspects of the two- and four-year colleges; and with cooperation and coordination among the various colleges. However, one cannot make judgments concerning the performance of the students independent of the context of the colleges in which they are enrolled and of the state systems (however loosely conceived) of which they are a part. The conclusions are in effect assessments or judgments based on the totality of the findings from both studies. They undoubtedly reflect certain values, primarily the point of view that society benefits from having its citizenry educated to its highest potential and that the junior college could be a powerful force in developing a much better educated citizenry. Somewhat different conclusions might be drawn from the findings by others with different points of view.

The implications pointed out here are primarily for action rather than further research. Many areas for study will be obvious from the discussion of findings; others will evolve as the changes and trends in higher education which have been enumerated become realities. However, throughout the discussion runs the thread of the continuing need for the two- and four-year colleges to know themselves and each other much more intimately than has ever been true before.

[1] The material on conclusions and implications is quoted directly from chapter 7 of the report of the second study, *Articulation Between Two-Year and Four-Year Colleges* (Berkeley: Center for the Study of Higher Education, University of California, 1964).

86

Conclusion. Junior colleges are making it possible for increasing numbers of high school graduates to begin work for baccalaureate degrees—students who would not otherwise be able to do so for reasons of academic or economic deficiency or for lack of family encouragement. The large number of successful teachers, engineers, businessmen, government workers, and other useful citizens who began their degree programs in two-year colleges is impressive.

Implications. The goal of equality of opportunity in higher education can be approached by expanding and strengthening the public community colleges and by providing them with adequate financial support while keeping tuition and other charges as low as possible. These open-door colleges should continue to be the melting pot of higher education, where every type of student has an opportunity to strive for the highest educational goal he believes he is capable of achieving. In the interests of both society and the individual, a higher proportion of college-age youth—perhaps most—should be enrolling in the two-year community colleges in the years immediately ahead.

Conclusion. The general public (including the parents of high school students) still tends to undervalue the contribution of the junior college to higher education and to view it as a kind of refuge for the "cannots," academically, and the "have nots," financially. The public votes for the establishment of new junior colleges and pays taxes to support them, but fails to recognize them as an appropriate institution for a majority of the high school graduates who seek two or more years of college education. Counselors, teachers, and parents are all prone to use the junior college as a kind of threat when college-bound students are not achieving as well as they should in high school. The fact that a very large percentage of state university graduates began their work in a two-year college is not sufficiently publicized nor is the record made by such students in competition with students who spent all four years in one institution. As a result, the junior college has been slow in coming into its own as a positive force in higher education.

Implications. Many states are now at some stage of creating master plans for higher education or of implementing plans which have recently been approved. Care is needed to identify the real role of the junior college in higher education in the plan for each state.

The four-year institutions must bear their share of the responsibility for helping the public understand the junior college role. All too often the junior college is pictured in master plans as the panacea for all ills and problems in higher education—increasing costs, mounting enrollment pressures, shortages of qualified faculty members for the four-year colleges. Locally, supporters promise much in trying to gain approval to establish new junior colleges, but then fail to carry on the public information function until such time as additional support is needed. Ways should be found to help the public understand both the potential of the junior college in higher education and the problems its creation sometimes brings. Hopefully the rapidly growing numbers of junior college graduates will become convincing interpreters of the role and functions of the junior college.

Conclusion. In attempting to expand opportunity at the lower division level and to strengthen education at the graduate level, master planners tend to assume that adequate educational opportunity between these two levels will be offered without any attention on their part to coordinated planning. The advantage gained by expanding opportunity in the junior colleges may well be negated by failure to provide new types of opportunity and additional spaces in existing upper division programs to accommodate the growing numbers of transfer students. It may be desirable to develop entirely new types of programs, in some cases by building on junior college occupational curricula as technology expands and in others by designing different levels of programs in such fields as engineering and business administration. As a two-year college program is rapidly becoming a requirement for many types of employment today, it is possible that within a matter of years a baccalaureate degree—perhaps in a two-plus-two program—will be a requirement in many new fields.

Implications. Master planners cannot afford to continue to neglect curriculum in the four-year colleges, if the increased numbers of students going to junior colleges are to be served. Many state colleges which offered only teacher education until recently are now evolving into multipurpose institutions, often at the university level. Conscious of their new status, they are prone to neglect their responsibilities to the junior colleges and, instead, try to copy the major state universities in curriculum development and standards or to develop unique programs which cannot be easily articulated with those of the junior colleges. The obligation of the four-year colleges to plan for the orderly accommodation of increasing numbers of transfer students should probably be made more explicit in state master plans which call for strengthened junior colleges. Coordinating agencies might undertake the development of undergraduate curriculum master plans at an early date to insure that new opportunities will be available as needed.

Conclusion. The door should be kept open to allow capable junior college students who are attracted into terminal occupational programs to transfer. One easy but undesirable solution to crowding in the four-year colleges is to exclude arbitrarily the junior college students who have enrolled in occupational programs designed to be terminal. Techniques for classifying students as "terminal" and "transfer" and for counseling them into appropriate programs are no better than existing techniques for matching student and college at the freshman level. Closing the door to the four-year colleges to good students in all nontransfer programs would result both in discouraging many capable students from enrolling in such programs and in denying opportunity to others who should go on to work for baccalaureate degrees.

Implications. It might be preferable to cease referring to programs as "terminal" and "transfer" and, instead, to recognize the student's right to be either terminal or transfer in either type of program, depending upon his achievement, abilities, and changing interests. As the four-year colleges become more selective at the freshman level, there will be increasing pressures to become selective in admitting students into junior college transfer programs. Consideration should be given to the question of whether the transfer "umbrella" for all nonvocational students is really appropriate.

Conclusion. All or most junior college students could be successful in achieving their degree goals after transfer *if* they would select four-year institutions and major fields which are appropriate to their ability and prior achievement. In every state there is probably at least one four-year college in which each transfer student with a C average in junior college could succeed if he is properly financed and motivated. However, a large number of students are transferring to inappropriate institutions, i.e., to colleges in which they have a very low proba-

89

bility of earning satisfactory grades and thus of achieving their baccalaureate degree objectives.

Implications. The proper matching of transfer student and institution at the upper division level is just as important a goal as the matching of high school graduate and institution at the freshman level. The former is probably even more important than the latter, since fewer mistakes in choice can be remedied during the junior and senior years in college, particularly when students fail. More information should be obtained on a continuing basis concerning the relative success of transfer students in different types of four-year colleges and programs. More effective ways of using such information need to be conceived in counseling and admissions programs. All too little is known about decision-making concerning college attendance and transfer by the students and their parents, with or without the help of counselors. Planners need to know why mistakes are made in choosing transfer institutions and how they might be avoided. On a more philosophic plane, there is a need to evaluate the extent to which both society and the students themselves can afford such mistakes within the context of preserving maximum freedom of opportunity for higher education.

Conclusion. A number of the major state universities are now admitting transfer students somewhat indiscriminately on the basis of barely satisfactory junior college grades, on the grounds that all such students must be given an opportunity to attempt programs of their own choosing. These same institutions are failing to evaluate the effects of their adoption of selective admission standards at the freshman level without an increase in standards for admission with advanced standing. The net result is an intensification of an existing problem by increasing the quality of the native students with whom the transfer students will have to compete for grades in the upper division.

Implications. There appears to be need for either higher (or selective) admission standards for transfer students or more effective admissions counseling, or both, if society is to be able to capitalize fully on the development of new opportunity in higher education through the junior college. It may be shortsighted to expand junior colleges which are committed to an open-door policy and then fail to take whatever steps are necessary to insure that transfer students from these colleges are admitted to institutions in which they can fulfill their degree goals. Both the master planners and the universities need to consider the right of the junior college graduate to transfer to *any* public four-year college. If opportunity to transfer to the major state universities is limited to those with a reasonable probability of success, the next question to be faced is the extent to which specialized majors should be developed in other types of institutions to which transfer students can be diverted.

Conclusion. The effects of diversity in higher education—in the quality of the entering students, level of instruction, types of programs, climate for learning, and pursuits of the faculty— are reflected in the findings concerning the differential performance of the transfer students. Because of the vast differences which were found among the forty-three four-year institutions which participated in the study, among the five types of such institutions, and among the ten states, no single meaningful conclusion can really be drawn about the quality of transfer student performance. Transfer students with very similar grades from the same junior college, often in the same field, will have quite different degrees of success in different four-year institutions, both in their persistence to graduation and their upper division grades. Diversity among institutions will probably increase as a function of greater statewide coordination and as institutions are encouraged to develop along particular lines to serve a specific clientele.

Implications. There is need to study the characteristics of the students who persist and graduate from different types of institutions, as well as the students who are admitted as freshmen. Colleges should analyze the composition, characteristics, and achievement of their graduating classes to find out what kinds of students are successful in their programs. It is false to assume that a junior college student with a C average will do equally well in all four-year institutions or in all programs, or that he will be able in all instances to compete successfully with native students who may have greater ability. To accommodate the heterogeneity of talent and interests which is present in the very large groups of junior college students who plan to transfer to four-year institutions, diversity of opportunity needs to be developed at the junior and senior levels.

Conclusion. The C grade and the C grade point average earned in junior college are relatively meaningless as indicators of a student's likelihood of success in four-year institutions. Grades of A and B are given in junior college as recognition of superior achievement, but a C grade may be given as a reward for compliance with course requirements at only a minimally acceptable level. In fact, the grade of C may be given with the thought that it will be discounted if the student applies for transfer. Naturally, a C grade may mean many things when given by different instructors to different students for different reasons. This is undoubtedly as it must be, but it would be a mistake to interpret C grades out of context.

Implications. A thoughtful assessment of the rational basis for assigning junior college grades is needed now, at a time when standards in the four-year colleges are rising and when the group to be served by the junior college is expanding rapidly. As the junior colleges attempt to accommodate an ever increasing percentage of high school graduates and to provide programs appropriate to their needs and abilities, the problem of the C grade becomes even more acute. The programs offered tend to be either vocational or transfer. Some students in each will be terminal while some in each will enter four-year institutions. The student with only moderate ability who has no interest in a vocational program will probably declare his intention to transfer in order to gain admission to a program in the liberal arts. The question then is posed: To whom should the junior college C grade be awarded for doing satisfactory work at a minimum level—to the student who aspires to transfer to a major university? to the terminal, nonvocational student with moderate ability? or to some faceless student between the two extremes?

The temptation has always been strong to tie junior college grades to those given by the major universities and to use the grade point differential as a basis for evaluating the success of transfer students. The junior colleges take pride in striving toward a zero differential with the universities; movement in this direction from year to year is regarded by them as improvement. As the junior colleges begin to serve a much broader segment of high school graduates, and as the universities become much more selective, this standard will be less appropriate than ever. Clearly the whole matter of grading in the two types of institutions is a necessary area for articulation at the state level.

Conclusion. Junior colleges are doing a more effective job in educating their good students, i.e., those who have aptitude for college work and good high school grades, than in preparing students with serious high school deficiencies for transfer to four-year institutions. Students with poor high school records who attend junior college with no intervening experience and earn only C grades while making up high school deficiencies, probably while working at least part-time, have less than an even chance of success after transfer to most four-year colleges.

Implications. A closer look needs to be taken at what have been termed the "late bloomers" in junior college to find out why some are successful after transfer and why so many others fail. Weak students with both subject-matter and scholarship deficiencies should probably remain in junior college for more than two years before transfer in order to catch up with their classmates who began junior college without such deficiencies. The real test of the weaker students' abilities to do satisfactory work at the baccalaureate degree level may then come in the last courses to be taken in junior college, which are too often postponed until after transfer by students who enter junior college with deficiencies. For such students a three-plus-two program would probably bring greater success than a two-plus-three program, from which many students are now being dropped one year after transfer because of poor grades.

Conclusion. There is so much overlap in the distribution of academic aptitude of the transfer students who graduate and those who drop out that test scores do not distinguish very efficiently among the successes and failures. If junior college grades are used appropriately in screening, counseling, and/or selecting transfer students for admission to particular institutions, there should be little need to introduce test results as further evidence of capacity to do satisfactory work in the upper division. This does not, of course, argue against the use of test results obtained for transfer students for other purposes nor does it deny a significant relationship between test scores and grade point averages. Some possible uses of test results at the time of transfer include placement in course sequences, demonstration of proficiency, qualification for honors programs, and validation of credit for courses for which transfer credit is not normally awarded.

Implications. Test results should probably not be used to deny admission to transfer students if their junior college grades are good and if their occupational goals are reasonable ones. A large number of high school graduates with considerably less ability than the average university freshman are succeeding in junior college and going on to four-year institutions where they earn baccalaureate degrees in many different fields. On the other hand, some students with more than average ability do poor work in high school, earn only barely satisfactory grades in junior college, and are poor candidates for upper division standing, at least in the major universities. It appears that many four-year institutions are able to accommodate transfer students with a very wide range of ability who persist through the lower division in junior college and who are motivated to transfer.

Conclusion. The average ability level of graduates who were freshmen in the major universities is higher than that of their counterparts who began their baccalaureate degree programs in two-year colleges, although there is considerable overlap in the ability of the students in the two types of colleges. Differences in their university grades reflect this difference in average ability, which is compounded by the often difficult academic and personal adjustment which the transfer students must make when they enter the university as juniors. When groups of comparable ability compete for grades in the upper division, as in the teachers colleges, the chances are good that the transfer students will earn grades which are as high as those of the native students. Few junior college students with high ability and good junior college grades are handicapped after transfer when competing with native students for grades which would qualify them for admission to graduate school.

Implications. When transfer students to particular institutions have less academic ability than native students, they should not be expected to earn grades on a par with those of the natives. The more important question to be answered is whether transfer students with lesser ability earn grades which enable them to persist and to meet graduation requirements. If the yardstick used to measure transfer student success is the grade point average earned by native students, without controlling for differences in academic aptitude, one may expect to find that junior college students will be required to meet ever increasing admission standards for transfer. Coordinating agencies should strive to maintain a good academic "mix" in the junior colleges, i.e., to avoid siphoning off all the best students for the four-year institutions. If the junior colleges are left to educate only the rejects from the four-year colleges, equality of opportunity will be lessened by the decline in quality of instruction which would ensue.

94

Conclusion. At least during their first year after transfer, grade point differentials are one of the realities of university life which transfer students to these institutions should be prepared to accept. However, junior college students are transferring to many different types of four-year colleges, with different grading standards and with varying differentials. Most students will suffer some drop in grades in their first semester after transfer, but the size of the drop and the degree of improvement afterward varies with the institution. A particular junior college will probably have a near zero differential with some institutions and a fairly sizeable negative differential with others, all within the same state. Significant positive differentials will be fairly rare and might be viewed with some concern as possible indicators of overly tough junior college grading standards.

Implications. Before attempting to evaluate and perhaps to tamper with its grading standards, each junior college should examine annually its grade point differentials with *each* four-year college to which a sizeable number of its students transfer. Because of the status factor, the temptation is strong to try to reduce the differential with the major state university to nearly zero, while ignoring differentials with other types of four-year colleges. However, any arbitrary attempt to close the gap with the major universities could result in the denial of opportunity to many transfer students who are now succeeding in various types of colleges. A more realistic goal is the achievement of a differential which most transfer students can "afford," i.e., a drop in grades which will not result in an average below C. Transfer students whose junior college average is only 2.3 can ill afford a differential of $-.5$; however, a group whose average is 2.8 could experience a drop in grades of this magnitude without fear of probation and dismissal.

If good junior college students are not alerted to the possibility that their grades will drop after transfer, they may become discouraged and even withdraw, though still in good standing. There is clearly no simple approach to evaluating grade point differentials or to bringing about desired changes in them, but it would be wise to view these differentials as very rough indicators of the appropriateness of both grading and admission standards in the two- and four-year colleges.

Conclusion. New junior colleges are offering educational opportunity to countless thousands of high school graduates of

95

average ability who have inadequate financial resources to attend a four-year college outside their home communities (or to pay tuition at local four-year institutions to which they might be admitted). Many are attracted to transfer programs in the junior colleges with the expectation of becoming engineers, teachers, and other types of professional workers, only to be stranded two years later with no more financial backing than they had when they graduated from high school. Others take jobs while enrolled in junior college in order to earn money for expenses after transfer and neglect their studies in doing so, although they are able to earn C grades which qualify them for transfer. Under present financial arrangements and programs, many junior college students are developing false expectations about transfer and are having to drop out after finding that they cannot solve their financial problems.

Implications. In the light of the needs of the students who begin their degree programs in junior colleges, a critical examination should be made both of the current philosophy of financial aid and of the nature of existing programs. Most of these students would not be regarded as contenders for scholarships. On the other hand, they are being encouraged to embark upon two-plus-two programs with at least a tacit assumption that some form of aid will be available to them to transfer if they do satisfactory work. Some of the questions which need to be examined are these: Should junior college students with only C averages be advanced money for their expenses in the upper division to be repaid after graduation (assuming that students with A's and B's are already being taken care of)? Should potential scholarship winners at the freshman level be encouraged to attend junior college with the promise of aid as juniors? Is the present trend toward greatly increased aid to capable high school graduates to enable them to enter four-year colleges as freshmen a wise one or should substantial sums be reserved for deserving transfer students at the junior level?

Conclusion. Counseling about college attendance and career choice needs to be greatly improved at all levels—high school, junior college, and in the four-year institutions. Counselors must become aware of the interdependence of the various levels and segments of education and of the need for long-range planning by the students. They must be alert to the varying patterns of attendance which many students now pursue in college —two-plus-two programs, employment between high school and college or during college, off-campus and part-time study leading into regular degree programs, and work-study curricula. Both counselors and teachers tend to be familiar with the colleges in which they received their own training but to be woefully uninformed about the many other institutions which their students may attend, particularly the new community colleges. The kinds of information which counselors, students, and their parents need to make intelligent choices and decisions about college are not yet clear but it is certain that the information presently available is vastly inadequate.

Implications. Improvements in counseling will come about only as a result of related actions on several fronts. First, college administrators and board members need to be convinced of the contribution which counseling could make to the total educational experience of the students, given adequate financial support and appropriately trained staff. Unless budget- and policy-makers recognize the need for increased support for counseling, the other changes will be relatively ineffective. The second strong need is for the upgrading of both pre-service and in-service training programs for counselors, particularly for the junior colleges. The goals and objectives of junior college counseling need to be defined more clearly as one basis for developing more appropriate counselor training programs. The needs of the transfer students for counseling services should be examined in the light of the new information from this study. The implication is *not* that counseling now being done is poor, but that there is not enough of it and that too few students are now benefiting from present counseling services.

Conclusion. In many four-year institutions transfer students are being overlooked in planning orientation programs, in offering counseling services to new students, in inviting their participation in social and extracurricular activities, and, above all, in giving appropriate academic advice at the time of their first registration. There was little or no evidence of discriminatory policies or practices affecting the junior college transfer students, but compared with the attention given the entering freshmen, there was a general lack of concern for their needs and interests. The new freshman continues to be the preferred client of the four-year institutions, and of their student services programs, while the transfer student is usually left to make his own adjustment to the new situation.

Implications. Before appropriate action with respect to the programs can be taken, the four-year colleges may need to look at the characteristics of their new undergraduate transfer groups—the number of students, their age, their class levels, the types of colleges they come from (and the reasons they transferred), their sex, their housing, and their interests. Too often the transfer students are grouped ignominiously with the new freshmen in orientation programs where they feel awkward and unwelcome. Their need for orientation may be different from that of the freshmen because of their college experience and greater maturity, but it is probably no less. Similarly, since many are still unsure of themselves or uncertain that their decisions have been the proper ones, their need for both counseling and academic advising is often acute during their first year after transfer. Special advisers in the four-year institutions may be needed who have a philosophical commitment to the junior college and who would make it their business to become well acquainted with the junior colleges which are the major sources of upper division transfer students.

Conclusion. The good performance of the students after transfer is consistent with their appraisal of the quality of instruction they received in the junior college. Well-qualified instructors who are deeply interested in students and in teaching are making it possible for the junior college to bridge the gap between the high school and the university. The very bright students who make this appraisal are undoubtedly correct in suggesting some changes, however. The somewhat slower pace which characterizes instruction in the junior college could be accelerated during the second year, with substantial benefits accruing to the students who intend to transfer to major universities in particular. Methods of instruction, techniques for evaluation, assignments of reading, and term papers—all these could be made to approximate university instruction somewhat more closely as the time approaches for the students to transfer.

Implications. Although one of the great fears of those who would strengthen junior colleges is that they will evolve into imitations of the major state universities, it seems desirable that cautious but deliberate attempts be made to "beef up" the instruction of the university-bound transfer students during their second year in junior college. This could be done without disturbing the essential character of junior college instruction as a bridge between high school and university. Since the numbers of students who transfer to the universities are usually quite large, it should be possible to arrange for some special work for them during their second year including, perhaps, special sections of some classes, added library and written assignments, varied types of testing, seminars, and other devices. Good students are now satisfied with their junior college education, as much as and perhaps more so than students who do only average work in junior college. To keep the former group in junior college and to educate them appropriately, ways of offering them accelerated instruction during their second year should be identified and implemented.

Conclusion. There is no reason why junior college transfer students should require more time and units than native students to complete their degree programs, if the two- and four-year colleges work together on problems of articulation of their courses and curricula. Junior college students may be older than their native counterparts when they finish their degrees for one or several reasons—high school deficiencies to be made up before starting college-level courses, exploration in junior college before choosing a major or transfer program, part-time enrollment or withdrawal while earning money to continue their education, and late decision to attend college. However, recent high school graduates who enter college without deficiencies and enroll on a full-time basis, who choose their major and transfer institution not later than the end of their freshman year, should be able to progress through their two-plus-two programs at the same rate of speed as their classmates in four-year institutions.

Implications. The junior college is and should remain essentially a two-year institution, offering approximately half the baccalaureate degree program. However, despite restrictions on the amount of credit which can be transferred to four-year colleges, most students should be urged to remain in junior college until they can transfer with full upper division standing, with all lower division requirements met, and with various prerequisites satisfied. While the situation was good when the 1960 group moved through their degree programs, it probably could be improved if the junior colleges would study the detailed performance records of their transfer students. An analysis of the records would in many instances reveal specific transfer problems which could be remedied quite easily, thus enabling an even larger number of transfer students to graduate on time and also avoiding the loss of some students who drop out lacking only some minor requirement which often could have been met in junior college.

Conclusion. Attrition after transfer, for all causes, is higher than it ought to be and could probably be reduced through joint efforts on the part of the two- and four-year colleges. Factors related to attrition are multiple and complex, but the reasons given by the transfer students for dropping out as juniors and seniors seem to have somewhat more validity than those given by most freshmen and sophomores who feel they must save face when withdrawing. Factors of unsatisfactory grades, financial instability, and insufficient motivation or interest frequently combine to produce withdrawal among the transfer students. Thus, the same factors which directed them to junior colleges as freshmen, rather than to four-year institutions, later bring about their withdrawal as juniors and seniors.

Implications. As noted previously, a sizeable reduction in attrition could be produced by means of a better matching of transfer students and four-year colleges, with the objective of getting each student into an institution where he has a better-than-even chance of success. However, unless a different approach is made to the administration of financial aid to transfer students, many who are now attempting to complete baccalaureate degree programs without adequate financial resources would be well advised to make other plans. Transfer to most four-year colleges involves a cash outlay of a totally different magnitude than junior college expenses. Many students are transferring with little or no family backing, very limited savings on which to draw, and no workable solution for financing their education beyond the first semester or year in the four-year college. The drop in grades which many experience after transfer makes them even less likely to be able to obtain the needed funds through part-time employment or assistance from the university.

One of the major reasons the students attend junior college as freshmen is their lack of motivation or uncertainty about their interests in or capability for baccalaureate degree programs. After transfer, many drop out for these same reasons. They complain about a lack of assistance from counselors and other staff members in working through their motivational problems, including frequent disappointment in their chosen major or profession, conflicting values, personal problems, and others. One possible implication is that the junior college should permit and perhaps encourage former students to return to talk through their problems with former counselors and instructors. In any event, the two-year investment which has been made in these transfer students could produce a much higher pay-off for them and for society if somewhat greater assistance in various forms were provided when they leave the junior college.

Conclusion. Present articulation machinery in many states and in many institutions is inadequate to solve the problems which will be brought on by an increasing volume of transfer students. Problems of numbers will be complicated by an increased diversity in the programs offered by the various four-year colleges and by changing patterns of transfer to different types of institutions. Uniformity of program is impossible to achieve in either the junior colleges or the four-year institutions and is probably undesirable even if it could be achieved. Differences will continue to exist in the structure and content of general education programs, in course placements and prerequisites, and in methods of instruction and materials. Junior colleges should not be expected to offer an infinite number of transfer programs to parallel those of all four-year institutions to which their students might transfer. Neither can the junior college assume that all their students will transfer to the major state university after which they have tended to model their programs. A multi-college approach at the state level is needed to achieve good articulation of the two- and four-year programs and to preserve the individual college's right to experiment and innovate as well as to protect the student's transfer credit.

Implications. Two- and four-year colleges are rapidly becoming interdependent with respect to the planned mobility of their undergraduate students. If a certain degree of autonomy in curricular matters is to be preserved, considerable attention must be given to the development of common policies and guidelines for transfer to which the various colleges in each state will subscribe. Unless there is a high degree of articulation, it may become necessary to institute comprehensive college testing programs. The results of such tests might be used to decide which junior college students should transfer to what institutions, what kinds of credit they should receive, and when they are ready to graduate. If junior college students are to continue to transfer freely, with no loss of time in completing their programs, cooperation at the state level in developing guidelines is essential.

The various findings and conclusions might be summarized this way: the junior colleges have made a fine record in preparing students to transfer to a very diverse group of four-year colleges and universities, but improvement in the record is still possible. At the conclusion of the studies the Esso Education Foundation provided one means of securing such improvement by supporting a series of conferences to disseminate the research findings and to develop guidelines for transfer. Still, the major benefits from both the research and the conferences will accrue only as continuing articulation activity is set in motion by the conferences or is furthered by them where programs are already under way. It has been said that articulation is both a process and an attitude. Of the two, attitude is perhaps the more important, for unless the parties involved undertake the solution of transfer problems in a context of interdependence and shared responsibility, obviously there will be no workable process.

PB-8875-1
5-34T